Teaching Writing
PRIMER

PETER LANG
New York • Washington, D.C./Baltimore • Bern
Frankfurt am Main • Berlin • Brussels • Vienna • Oxford

P.L. Thomas

Teaching Writing
PRIMER

PETER LANG
New York • Washington, D.C./Baltimore • Bern
Frankfurt am Main • Berlin • Brussels • Vienna • Oxford

KH

Library of Congress Cataloging-in-Publication Data
Thomas, P. L. (Paul Lee).
Teaching writing primer / P.L. Thomas.
p. cm.
Includes bibliographical references.
1. English language—Composition and exercises—Study and teaching.
2. Language arts. 3. Critical pedagogy. I. Title.
LB1576.T52   372.62'3—dc22   2004026587
ISBN 0-8204-7842-3

Bibliographic information published by **Die Deutsche Bibliothek**.
Die Deutsche Bibliothek lists this publication in the "Deutsche
Nationalbibliografie"; detailed bibliographic data is available
on the Internet at http://dnb.ddb.de/.

Cover design by Lisa Barfield

The paper in this book meets the guidelines for permanence and durability
of the Committee on Production Guidelines for Book Longevity
of the Council of Library Resources.

Printed in the United States of America

8/26/05

Table of Contents

Introduction

Regardless of the age or experience of the student or the expertise and training of the teacher, teaching writing offers both student and teacher considerable struggles; the phrase itself holds pitfalls in each word: "teaching" and "writing." With performances such as writing (and with playing a sport, creating art, and so forth), "teaching" is often less direct (as I will discuss in Chapter Three) and more synonymous with coaching, fostering, or mentoring although I am driven to add that the teaching of writing does occasionally require direct instruction.

"Learning to write is a matter of learning to shatter the silences, of making meaning, of learning to learn," Maxine Greene (1995) proclaims, reminding us of the personal and academic values of writing as an act and as a form of expression and communication. Writing is both expression and discovery. And while Greene's insight is true about the power and challenges of learning to write, learning to teach writing may be even more daunting.

Writing is a performance just as playing soccer is a performance; a writing teacher, like a soccer coach, has to observe and offer advice while the novice writer *writes*. "Writing" as a term is more problematic; often teachers who deal with literacy use "writing" interchangeably to mean "creating text by handwriting or typing" ("Jessica writes on the walls in her bedroom") and "composing sentences and paragraphs to create and share meaning with an audience" ("Jessica likes to write in her journal, but she doesn't enjoy writing essays in school"). For this discussion, then, we will focus on *teaching writing* to mean the following: *To foster composing in students of all ages for purposeful expression to an audience.*

This introduction addresses the broad implications inherent in literacy instruction—the personal and social contexts of writing—along with the theories of learning and language acquisition that best support the teaching of writing. Chapter Two will trace the history of writing instruction and research to establish a framework of the perennial tensions that still exist in English/Language Arts (ELA) classrooms today. Next, I will explain how to implement a writing program in the classroom throughout Chapter Three—including best practice explanations of writing workshops, assessing writing, writing instruction, dealing with the paper load, writing forms, and the writing process. Since **high-stakes testing** and **accountability** currently swamp and corrupt most of the instruction taking place today, Chapter Four will dissect the dangers posed to writing instruction by **standardized testing** at the state and national levels. Chapter Five will explore the need for, and the advantages of, teachers of writing being writers themselves. A final chapter will offer references and resources for further exploration of the teaching of writing.

high-stakes testing

These tests are often gate keepers, determining grade promotion, course credit, graduation, or scholarships.

accountability

Systems and policies that include standards and formal assessments that measure and report student achievement for the purposes of improving teaching and learning, and for the purposes of holding students and teachers responsible for that teaching and learning.

standardized testing

Assessments that have standardized formats and purposes over large populations of test takers. These assessments are often highly regulated for validity and reliability.

Writing to Learn, Writing to Express, Writing to Be Free

Within every field and all that we teach, there exist larger issues—some at the surface and some less apparent. The teaching of writing shares a quality with all literacy education that cannot be ignored: language and power are inextricable. If we are addressing writing with our students, we are also addressing their empowerment.

Paulo Freire (1993) places a primary importance on literacy education in his discussion of the larger issues of education; literacy equals individual empowerment equals individual freedom. To discuss the teaching of writing, we have to consider writing as an act of learning, as an act of expression, and as an act of **empowerment** (Freedman et al., 1995). Central to that discussion is Freire's warning concerning prescription:

> One of the basic elements of the relationship between oppressor and oppressed is *prescription*. Every prescription represents the imposition of one individual's choice upon another, transforming the consciousness of the person prescribed to into one that conforms with the prescriber's consciousness. Thus, the behavior of the oppressed is a prescribed behavior, following as it does the guidelines of the oppressor. (pp. 28–29)

Freire recognizes that when teaching drifts into an act of prescription—as is often the case with writing instruction—the self-determination of the student is squelched. What I am seeking is a writing program that addresses writing well while also protecting the self-determination of each student.

The purpose of this book is to focus on the fostering of composing in students for expression and empowerment; while writing to learn is an integral part of both writing and learning, it will essentially be left to the fringes of our explorations. Freire's concern for the oppression inherent in prescription will ground the discussion of the teaching of writing, since it is my assertion that it is *not* an act of prescribing but rather one of empowerment.

Let's consider for a moment how Freire's warning about prescription currently looks in classrooms where students write, keeping in mind that this snapshot is typical of how writing has been taught in schools throughout the twentieth century. Most student-written essays are driven by a **prompt**; that prompt is at the heart of what Freire would call a pre-

empowerment
involves those qualities that allow a person to be self-directed with the least amount of coercion possible from some imposing authority.

prompt
A prompt is a statement that directs a student to perform a composition or a performance, generally for assessment. Most prompts provide the basic guidelines for the act, including topic, purpose, structure, and length.

scription. A typical school essay prompt would read: "Write an essay of 750–1000 words that analyses how irony and characterization contribute to the themes in Kate Chopin's 'The Story of an Hour.'" Behind the prescriptive nature of that prompt lurks even more damning dynamics. This prompt will have been preceded by the teacher *telling* students what the irony, characterization, and themes are. Essentially, school writing is characterized by prescriptive prompts that basically elicit recall by students who transcribe what they have been told in the format they have been told to follow.

Writing as human expression and writing as a performance of understanding are characterized by the sensitive and vital nature of writing, of composing. Similar to Freire's warnings, Greene (1995) supports the delicate nature and the value of writing:

> It is when I experience those forces as inhibiting, demeaning, and interfering with my freedom, that I am moved very often to *tell* about them. . . . It is by writing that I often manage to name alternatives and to open myself to possibilities. That is what I think learning ought to be. (p. 107)

Writing encompasses more than we often acknowledge as teachers of writing in school, but this text will explore writing for all that it is—an act of individual discovery and empowerment as well as a formal contribution to the social discourse of being a human.

Historically, a small number of people had a voice in any society—both the access and the right to make public statements. In most societies, discourse has been a moot point; in our democracy, access to expression and access to learning literacy skills are vital issues. The teaching of writing is a contribution to both the dignity of each student and the vitality of a culture. Further, I will discuss the teaching of writing as a pivotal goal of education since writing is an essential process in academic settings as a performance of understanding.

That grounding will provide a foundation as the larger purposes of writing instruction are explored; writing, by its nature, is both highly personal and uniquely idiosyncratic while simultaneously being bound by social obligations and contexts. Freire's concerns support several questions that are inherent in this book; these questions will remain for all writing teachers throughout their careers.

1. How does a teacher teach writing without drifting into **indoctrination**?
2. What assumptions about writing are inherent in the teacher's instruction, and how might those assumptions be made clear to all students?
3. How does the teacher balance student empowerment with social expectations and social conventions that impact written expression?

These questions serve as guiding concerns throughout my discussion, but they also serve as models of the need for **reflection** and **metacognition** as integral parts of the teaching process.

The teaching of writing, then, must be an act of discovery by the student, not a prescription imposed by a teacher onto the student. Yet, that act of discovery is necessarily accompanied by the social contexts in which she lives. Achieving a balance between the sacred nature of individual student empowerment and social constraints is a constant struggle in teaching writing.

indoctrination
The forcing of a learner to accept what is taught without input from that learner or without giving him the option of rejecting that learning is indoctrination.

reflection
As a teaching or learning tool, reflection is the act of thinking about one's actions or thoughts and providing a self-analysis of those acts or thoughts.

metacognition
Often referred to as "thinking about thinking." It involves gaining awareness about one's own thoughts and one's own thinking processes.

Learning Theory and Teaching Writing

As with all teaching, instruction is guided by a **theory of learning**—whether the teacher is completely conscious of the theory or not. Pervasive in most teaching throughout American schools is **behaviorism** as a learning theory. This theory has several elements that make it unsuitable for teaching writing, because it both violates many of Freire's conditions for learning for empowerment and inhibits a student from learning a performance through discovery. A more effective and more conducive learning theory for teaching writing is **constructivism** (Calfee, 1994b). The two will be contrasted in the following paragraphs to explore the disadvantages of behaviorism and the advantages of constructivism in a writing program.

theory of learning
Organized bodies of explanations for how people learn are generally called theories of learning.

behaviorism
Focuses primarily on those actions and results that can be observed and measured.

constructivism
Focuses on the inner working of learning.

Brooks and Brooks (1999) and Constance Weaver (1996) are typical of many educational theorists and practitioners who argue that constructivist learning theory is more suitable for writing instruction than the traditional assumptions of behaviorism. Behavioristic assumptions dominate most instruction in schools; for writing instruction to be effective and **emancipatory**, a learning theory **paradigm shift** must occur.

While this primer doesn't allow the space to consider both learning theories fully, let's establish a broad distinction between behaviorism and constructivism as scientifically grounded learning theories. Behaviorism characterizes learning as an act from outside the learner that creates learning through **stimulus/response** assumptions. At a simplistic level, behaviorism requires that the teacher has predetermined the goal of learning and that she use **positive reinforcement** to encourage students who work properly toward that goal and **negative reinforcement** to stop behaviors not conducive to learning what is required. A teacher who offers candy to students during a review for a test is practicing behavioristic assumptions that the rewards will result in her students learning the content.

Constructivism assumes that authentic learning develops from inside the student. The term itself is a metaphor for the basic concept; new learning is constructed on the foundation of earlier understandings. A teacher who asks students to do a quick journal entry about a time they were frightened as a pre-reading activity for an Edgar Allan Poe story is practicing constructivist learning theory by helping students activate their prior knowledge about being frightened, which should provide a platform for understanding Poe's writing.

Since American public education is dominated by behavioristic assumptions about teaching and learning, the following paradigm shifts will have to occur before writing instruction can be practiced effectively.

Teaching must move from part-to-whole instruction (behaviorism) to whole-to-part instruction (construc-

---

emancipatory

Those acts in education that assist either learners or teachers in gaining their self-direction are emancipatory.

---

paradigm shift

Occurs when a person moves from one model (paradigm) to another.

---

stimulus/response

In behavioristic learning theory, the stimulus is the act, often by the teacher, that causes some response in the learner.

---

positive reinforcement

Rewards for valued behaviors .

---

negative reinforcement

Punishments for discouraged behaviors.

tivism). Particularly when we are dealing with new or complex learning, teachers feel that learning is always improved if the larger body of learning is broken down into the smallest possible parts. This "gut feeling" turns out to be terribly flawed. Brain research indicates that the large majority of people are naturally **global learners**, not **analytic learners**; more than 75% of a class will learn best from whole-to-part. This came to light for me over many years of teaching poetry. I found that students tended to *first* offer what a poem means—before they could explain the smaller details of the poem or the evidence that builds to support that meaning.

This shift does not include ignoring part-to-whole learning. What is needed is *beginning* with whole-to-part instruction, which uncovers the smaller portion of students who need part-to-whole and facilitates helping the global learners gain analytical skills.

global learners

Value having the big picture first and often need direct help with breaking that concept into its component parts.

analytic learners

Naturally prefer that a larger concept or process be broken into its essential parts and organized from first to last.

Teaching must move from a linear, step-by-step assumption for all processes (behaviorism) to a holistic and chaotic model (constructivism). Another grand but flawed assumption is that learning is enhanced not only by breaking down the material but also by forcing all learning into a sequence. The problem here is, as noted above, learning is not necessarily enhanced by the large concept being reduced to pieces; often larger concepts can be broken into component parts, but that doesn't insure that these parts function in any given order.

As I will explore more fully later in this discussion, the writing process is typical of this problem. The process a writer practices to move from ideas to published writing does have identifiable aspects—traditionally labeled prewriting, drafting, revising, editing, finalizing, and publishing. Yet that process is actually unique to each writer and more chaotic than linear in nature. Outside the writing field, we often see students reflect the hidden message we send them about false order; they will explain something like the "four causes of the Civil War" and proceed to write "first," "second," etc., as if the events we call history occurred with the order and clarity that we often have in hindsight.

Teaching must move from an imposed curriculum (behaviorism) to a curriculum that begins with the student (constructivism). Most formal schooling proceeds with the assumption that what is to be learned—the **curriculum**—can be identified fairly easily and should be imposed onto the student. Constructivist learning theory believes that curriculum is both something to be discovered by the students and the teacher along with being debatable. The writing curriculum must be something each student discovers and creates through rich experiences; if a predetermined writing goal is imposed onto the student, the value in writing—as characterized earlier by Freire and Greene—is destroyed.

curriculum

The content, or what students learn

Teaching must move from teacher-centered classes (behaviorism) to student-centered classes (constructivism). Traditional schooling is teacher driven. The teacher determines what is to be learned, how it is to be learned, and what degrees of learning have taken place. For a successful writing program to develop, classes need to move towards becoming student centered. That would mean that most of the decisions currently in the hands of teachers—such as the topic and form of every writing assignment—must be moved into the hands of the students. This shift not only better respects the dignity of free people; it also adds needed complexity to the learning process.

Student-centered teaching and learning brings greater rigor to the curriculum since they ask students to make decisions that both increase and portray their understandings better. For example, a student who can write a prescribed essay—where the topic, the form, and the content are given by the teacher—is being asked to do far less than students who are required to consider what to discuss and how to discuss it. The student-centered classroom requires students to learn to be self-directed by actually being self-directed while under the helpful eye of an expert teacher.

Teaching must move from textbooks and worksheets (behaviorism) to authentic texts and student performances (constructivism). The predetermined nature of traditional classes lends itself to a prepackaged curriculum in the form of textbooks and worksheets. While this approach is often more manageable for teachers, it can contribute to many of the causes of weak student achievement—passive students performing prescribed and inauthentic tasks. The constructivist classroom exposes students to **authentic texts** and **primary documents**; students are asked to respond in authentic ways to these texts and ideas. In a history class, students would read the actual writing of Thomas Jefferson instead of a **synoptic text**'s explanation of his writing. Having to read and interpret Jefferson's ideas is far more challenging than ingesting the interpretation supplied for the student in a textbook.

Teaching must move from selected-response assessment (behaviorism) to created-response and performance assessment (constructivism). How teachers assess learning can often send the strongest messages to students. American society and the momentum of American education value highly a certain form of assessment that appears objective—**selected-response assessment**. Multiple-choice tests and their many cousins have several characteristics that actually are less challenging than assessment should be; as the name "selected response" implies, information is already on the assessment instrument and students simply choose. On selected-response assessment tests the chance always exists that students merely guess correctly. Particularly in writing instruction, students need to be assessed through **created-response assessments** and **performance assessments**—in other words, being assessed as writers by writing, both as a performance and an assessment.

Teaching must move from a drive to avoid student error (behaviorism) to embracing student error as a natural and necessary component to learning and discovery (constructivism). In most classes, whether on formal assessments or during question-and-answer sessions,

authentic texts

Works published for real-world purposes are authentic texts, in contrast with textbooks that are often written for a narrow and somewhat artificial purpose.

primary documents

Text written for an authentic purpose—as opposed to someone else's explanation of the original author's ideas.

synoptic text

A text written primarily to summarize large bodies of information

selected-response assessments

Assessments that require students to choose answers already provided on the test.

created-response assessments

Assessments that ask students to produce original work or performances.

performance assessments

Assessments or tests that have students perform some authentic act such as writing, singing, or playing a sport.

offering an incorrect answer carries either a numer-
ical or social punishment. If you dare to be wrong,
you are punished. Another hidden curriculum element in behavioristicly grounded classes is that we
should all avoid making errors. Constructivism
argues that errors and missteps actually are necessary
in the quest for understanding. A writing class must
create an atmosphere where experimentation is valued, where risk taking is a key element of the process,
and where the student-teacher dynamic is one of community instead of students looking to the teacher for
punishment and rewards. For example, if teachers can
begin giving credit on assessments instead of subtract-
ing credit—this means beginning all assessments
with zero, not one hundred and acknowledging
what students do well—then students begin to
embrace the potential of their learning instead of
dwelling on their errors.

*Teaching must move from being answer oriented (behav-
iorism) to being question oriented (constructivism).*
Particularly when we have discussions in classes, I
call the traditional process "Guess what the teacher
wants you to say"; it strikes me that most question-
and-answer sessions in classrooms look like trainers
tossing fish at the domesticated dolphins. The effective writing classroom will move away from seeking
the perfect and correct answers to an atmosphere of
continual skepticism; the world of scholarship is a
world of asking, not a static world of answers. This
is a difficult trend to overcome since the popular perception of knowledge is best reflected in game shows
such as *Jeopardy!* or *Who Wants to Be a Millionaire?*
Yet, this transition can be aided if, as a teacher, you
begin to drive your teaching each day by questions
instead of behavioral objectives—keeping in mind
that the most effective questions are open ended, thus
having either no clear answers or a wide array of possible legitimate answers.

*Teaching must move from depending on external moti-
vation such as punishments and rewards (behaviorism)
to fostering internal motivation (constructivism).* Recently

I watched a review session in a middle school ELA class; as the teacher reviewed literary terms, students were tossed candy if they answered correctly. The students were answering for the candy. The knowledge of literary terms was lost in the dust of getting a Jolly Rancher! From candy to grades, students are trained to value some external thing over the value in the learning experience itself. Writing instruction must be driven by the value inherent in self-expression; this can be fostered only if student choices in content and form are valued and practiced (I will explore this more fully later). External motivation as the default approach to teaching and as a necessity for learning is terribly flawed and antithetical to a democratic way of life, to the potential of a free, self-governing people. There are intrinsic values to these things that are authentic; that authenticity must be the goal of our classes.

Teaching must move from an academic/theoretical perspective (behaviorism) to a contextual/pragmatic perspective (constructivism). As a continuation of the point above, the behavioristic model for learning and teaching creates a school setting that tends to be highly theoretical and merely academic. As I will discuss later, the typical essay form assigned in school is found essentially only in narrow academic settings. The five-paragraph essay and the thesis-driven essay are not authentic, not the stuff of professional writing. I could make a rather long list of other examples, but let me simply say that much of what we do in school is justified only because *we do it in school.* This circular justification for imposing learning templates for performances and selected-response assessments needs to be exposed and resoundingly rejected.

While a shift away from behavioristic assumptions is needed in all schooling, I believe, there are many justifications for making this paradigm shift in writing instruction. The constructivisticly based writing classroom assumes that language is a natural human performance although it recognizes that speaking and listening are natural while reading and writing are somewhat arbitrary systems humans have created from those natural behaviors. Constructivist learning theory also supports both the sacred nature of the individual (each person can learn and deserves the opportunity to make his or her own decisions) and the reality of social constraints (organizations and entities of any kind can gravitate toward discounting individual wants and even rights).

Everyone is born with the right to pursue life, liberty, and happiness, but the choices each person makes must be informed choices guided by an awareness of the consequences of those choices. Simply put, students must realize that choosing a topic for writing and choosing the form that the writing will take will be interpreted and evaluated by an audience with assumptions and prejudices guiding these interpretations and evaluations. All writers must be aware of the conventions and expectations within the field and within the audience that will read their compositions; each writer must evaluate to what degree she will conform to or reject those conventions, gauging how likely her piece is to be effective within those parameters. If I am a journalist, I may not succeed long, if at all, if I prepare my weekly column as a sonnet—but I certainly can take that risk if I am prepared to be resoundingly rejected by my audience and even my editor.

With this chapter's discussion in mind, in Chapters Two and Three I will discuss the behavioristic assumptions that have corrupted writing instruction throughout the greater part of the last 100 years, and I will highlight the greater effectiveness of writing instruction that shifts from an imposition and template model to a workshop approach that uses real-world writing as models for students to discover themselves as writers. Along with the larger issue of literacy instruction as an act of empowerment and the impact of learning theory on writing instruction, we need to support writing instruction with the most current understandings of how humans acquire language.

Language Growth from the Inside Out

Teaching students to write has changed very little since the days when most writing instruction consisted of having students copy long passages from the Bible; in essence, practices have not changed at all. More often than not, we teach writing and language acquisition in general with the assumption that learning language is purely an act of mimicry. Yet, over the past 100 years, linguists have discovered a great deal about how humans develop linguistically, and what we now know to be true is in stark contrast with our previous assumptions. For our purposes, throughout this text, we will build upon what I consider to be an extension of the work of Noam Chomsky, whose essential writings have been refined and popularized by Steven Pinker (1994).

Pinker explains that Chomsky questioned the hold behaviorists had on scientific explanations for human behavior by noting two key points about human language use: first, "a language cannot be a repertoire of responses" since each manifestation of language is unique (Pinker notes the use of "goed" in children is not learned by mimicry—as in a child saying, "He goed with me yesterday."); and second, the early development of language—unique constructions—happens without formal instruction (p. 22). Brain research and other scientific explorations of human language development have increasingly supported the likelihood that language development is heavily pre-wired. Mimicry and memorization play some small roles in learning to write, but the basic grammar exists at birth in humans and needs to be fostered, not imprinted.

While natural language acquisition refers to speaking and listening, reading and writing instruction is most effective when these artificial behaviors are fostered from those natural bases. In other words, too much writing instruction is imposed upon students as if they have no basis for composing when in fact the great majority of humans have a wealth of linguistic skills inherent in their brains from which to work. It is significant that Pinker and other linguists and teachers of writing (i.e., Weaver, 1996) support the need for writing instruction to grow from the grammar and usage systems that already exist in the human brain.

Broadly stated, language acquisition theory must be re-examined and re-applied, just as learning theory must be reconsidered, for writing instruction to be effective. Currently, it appears that essential linguistic abilities are pre-wired in humans and that language acquisition is quite natural and relatively easy for very young children in the right circumstances—ones that are linguistically rich and which fulfill basic human needs for food, shelter, affection, and safety. The reading and writing systems that have been created are artificial and often illogical (Williams, 1990), so greater direct instruction is needed in order to excel in reading and writing. What I will discuss here is how this direct instruction looks to foster writers in authentic and dignified ways.

Toward a Revision of Teaching Writing

Teaching writing in an authentic and empowering way is the goal of this book. Constructivist learning theory and research on writing instruction and language acquisition will guide all the approaches discussed here. Many of these practices are still not typical in classrooms throughout America. With that in mind, I am suggesting a revision of teaching writing and a reconsideration of a number of central concepts to writing instruction. These central concepts include the following:

writing process

Includes several components: prewriting, drafting, revising, editing, submitting, and publishing.

- The **writing process**, which has come to be seen as a linear process including prewriting, drafting, editing, and publishing; here, we will argue that the writing process is actually chaotic—something that each writer must find for herself, not something that can be prescribed (Weaver, 1996, p. 83).

writing forms

Prose and poetry are the two broad categories of writing forms. Prose is driven by sentence and paragraph formation, while poetry is driven by line and stanza formation.

- **Writing forms**, such as the traditional essay, have been portrayed in traditional classrooms as templates—an artificial, paint-by-numbers approach to writing that exists in classrooms, but not in the real world. Students are better served to question the introduction-body-conclusion template (and the inherent thesis prerequisite) in contrast to the many and varied forms writing takes within the wide range of genres employed by practicing writers.

writing workshops
A classroom strategy and instruction process that allows class time for students to perform all the components of the writing process.

■ The **writing workshop** will be encouraged as a guiding classroom structure, as this workshop strategy encourages an on-going community of writers that is supportive and more authentic than a series of disjointed writing assignments (See Atwell, 1998, and the recommendations of the National Writing Project [www.writingproject.org] and the National Council of Teachers of English [www.ncte.org]).

■ Additional issues in writing instruction will be discussed more fully in the following chapters; for example, the paper load and writing assessment.

Of Grammar and Correcting Student Work

prescriptive grammar
Grammarians who attempt to preserve a certain set of language standards and who offer judgment on the relative correctness of language use.

In his broader discussions of education, Jacques Barzun (1991) noted that students could never learn to write by doing grammar worksheets and exercises; he knew that students needed to write to learn writing. He also acknowledged the many obstacles to having students write enough in classes—notably class size and the lack of teachers who were also writers. Nonetheless, he called for more writing by students. Embedded in this recognition that we have historically asked students to write far too rarely are ELA teachers' attitudes toward grammar and student errors.

descriptive grammar
Grammarians who embrace the evolving nature of grammar are engaging in descriptive grammar.

grammar
The system that guides the use of language.

Weaver (1996) and Williams (1990), among many other leaders in the field of writing, explain that the teaching of writing is greatly improved when teachers shift their grammatical stance from prescriptive to descriptive; the world of **prescriptive grammar** varies greatly from the world of **descriptive grammar**, particularly as they impact classroom instruction of writing. **Grammar**, **mechanics**,

mechanics
The marking system used in written language to assist in the making of meaning.

usage

Covers diction (word choice) and syntax (word order) in terms of how language is used within the confines of the grammar system.

Standard English

The agreement the users of English have for forming and formatting language use.

and **usage** standards do exist, but the history of written English has proven to be a dynamic system. In other words, the language changes, and so do the standards. Further, there is no need or value in attempting to stop language from changing. Young writers are better served learning that language is a living system, not a frozen set of rules. Many note that Shakespeare coined words and phrasing never seen before in the language; Shakespeare's English would be considered "wrong" in many ways if today's standards were imposed on his use of double negatives and emphatic constructions such as "more better."

A descriptive stance concerning **Standard English** is more honest and more conducive to fostering empowered young writers. As Weaver (1996) warns, students are more successful when the writing teacher suggests strategies for revising a piece of writing rather than simply marking all the mistakes. I will discuss this in greater depth later, but focusing on a need to comply (or not) with the standards of English is best left to the final stages of writing, after a valuable draft with meaningful expression has been crafted and when the writer feels justified in submitting a work for assessment or publication.

Closely examining our assumptions about Standard English aids our greater purpose for teaching writing, which is empowerment. bell hooks (1994), author and educator, speaks openly about wrestling with the potential and real dangers of dominant language systems to oppress. She sees the need for writing instruction to assist all people in a free society to make the dominant dialect their own; as hooks notes from an Adrienne Rich poem, the disempowered often must use the language of the dominant forces in a society to express themselves.

Finally, why a primer on teaching writing? I see three reasons. First, my experience as a writing teacher at the high school level and as a lead instructor with an affiliate of the National Writing Project (NWP) during my 20 years as an educator has taught me that most teachers have little or no direct instruction in teaching writing—though many desire such training. Next, teachers are currently under a double-edged sword that is calling for more and better writing instruction while ironically jeopardizing the conditions under which such instruction can occur. For example, the College Board, through the SAT and state accountability systems, is requiring original writing by students though research shows that such assessments also negatively impact writing instruction and the quality of student writing (Hillocks, 2003; Mabry, 1999; Freedman, 1995). Third, and most importantly, students in a free society deserve and must have the most empowering literacy education we can offer. Writing equals power, both for the individual and for society.

Reconsidering the Discussion So Far

critical theory
Calls for a skeptical stance and questions the balance of power in any interaction.

The nature of **critical theory** creates an interesting tension, if not outright irony. If I am asking you to take out your suitcase for teaching writing, to unpack it, to look over all that's there, and to repack it—possibly with the contents much changed—why should you listen unflinchingly to my assumptions and arguments? That is a valid question, one that suggests that the unpacking and repacking are at least as important as the process and what you travel with each day to your writing classes.

Of course, throughout this primer, I am asserting what I believe to be the most effective avenues to quality writing instruction. But my arguments are made with one grand assumption: Things Change. I am certain we have a better understanding of how humans learn, how language is acquired, and how writing is best taught—today. I am also certain that what we do in our classes has lagged behind these more sophisticated understandings. Throughout the course of this book, I am asking that you use my lens to reconsider and to make a commitment to teaching writing as well as you can while keeping several concerns close at hand.

- What are my evolving assumptions about learning, and how do they impact my teaching and the learning of my students?

- What are my evolving assumptions about how language is acquired and how writing is learned, and how do they impact my teaching and the learning of my students?
- How can I be the most effective teacher possible while respecting above all else the dignity, humanity, and empowerment of my students?
- How can I be always a student—even while being a teacher, a writer, and a fellow human to those I teach?

Before moving to the next chapter, let's return to the voice that begins this chapter. Greene (1995) has cautioned: "As a set of techniques, literacy has often silenced persons and disempowered them. Our obligation today is to find ways of enabling the young to find their voices, to open their spaces, to reclaim their histories in all their variety and discontinuity" (p. 120). We will continue this exploration of teaching writing by looking at the history and research of writing instruction.

Glossary

accountability—Systems and policies that include standards and formal assessments that measure and report student achievement for the purposes of improving teaching and learning and for the purposes of holding students and teachers responsible for that teaching and learning. Examples include state standards, state tests for grade promotion of graduation, school report cards, and federal legislation such as No Child Left Behind.

analytic learners—Brain research and research into learning have found that about 20–25% of learners naturally learn new information from part-to-whole, and often benefit from experiencing that learning sequentially. Analytic learners would naturally prefer that a larger concept or process be broken into its essential parts and organized from first to last. These learners would assemble a new bicycle by following the written or graphic directions provided by the manufacturer.

authentic texts—Works published for real-world purposes are authentic texts; in contrast with textbooks that are often written for a narrow and somewhat artificial purpose. A basic example would be contrasting a picture book for children (authentic text) with a reading primer that overtly teaches reading through literature and exercises provided in the text. Further, a biography of Thomas Jefferson (authentic text) stands as a contrast with a U. S. history textbook that summarizes the whole of U. S. history.

behaviorism—As a learning theory, behaviorism focuses primarily on behavior—those actions and results that can be observed and measured. According to behaviorism, teaching and learning are essentially described as a series of stimuli and responses managed by the teacher to elicit desired behaviors, and thus learning, in the student. Simply put, behaviorism as a learning theory begins with a given curriculum (what students are to learn) and the teacher provides rewards for student behaviors leading to that goal and punishments to dissuade students who are not conforming to the goal. The use of grades is a basic example of behavioristic learning theory in traditional classrooms.

constructivism—As a learning theory, constructivism focuses on the inner working of learning. This theory embraces that humans are primarily equipped to learn and that much of the human mind already includes platforms for learning to be built upon, or constructed from the inside out. As humans absorb the world around them, they are continually building ever-evolving understandings of the world. The focus, unlike behaviorism, is not on that which is only observable or measurable; thus constructivist learning theory relies on a broader range of measurements than behaviorism.

created-response assessments—Assessments that ask students to produce original work or performances are created-response assessments. Short-answer or essay questions on an exam are two examples.

critical theory—While not easily explained or defined, critical theory in education often includes a concern for the social dynamics of education, and the impact of institutional assumptions on learning and teaching. Broadly, critical theory calls for a skeptical stance and questions the balance of power in any interaction. As a result, critical theory encourages dialogue and reflection by everyone involved in education.

curriculum—The content, or what students learn, is the curriculum. Traditionally, the act of educating involves the what (curriculum) and the how (instruction), in conjunction with measuring the effectiveness of both (assessment).

descriptive grammar—Grammarians who embrace the evolving nature of grammar are engaging in descriptive grammar. They see their work as describing the current state of grammatical standards while avoiding judging the correctness of such.

emancipatory—Those acts in education that assist either learners or teachers in gaining their self-direction are emancipatory.

empowerment—In education, who has authority and how that
authority is practiced are both crucial concerns. Empowerment
involves those qualities that allow a person to be self-
directed with the least amount of coercion possible from some
imposing authority.

global learners—Brain research and research into learning have
shown that 75–80% of learners naturally learn from whole-
to-part. Global learners value having the big picture first and
often need direct help with breaking that concept into its
component parts. These learners will often set aside the man-
ufacturers directions for assembling the bicycle and work from
the picture on the box.

grammar—The system that guides the use of language is called
grammar. In the narrowest sense, grammar encompasses issues
such as parts of speech, agreement, and other issues per-
taining to how spoken and written language are organized.

high-stakes testing—One component of the accountability movement has been testing that is "high stakes." These tests are
often gate keepers, determining grade promotion, course
credit, graduation, or scholarships. Examples include state
exams linked to standards, or the SAT when linked to college entrance or scholarships.

indoctrination—The forcing of a learner to accept what is taught
without input from that learner or without the option of rejecting that learning is indoctrination.

mechanics—The marking system used in written language to assist
in the making of meaning is generally called mechanics. This
area includes the use of commas, periods, quotation marks,
and such.

metacognition—Metacognition is often referred to as "thinking
about thinking." It involves gaining awareness about one's
own thoughts and one's own thinking processes.

negative reinforcement—Punishments for discouraged behaviors
are the most common negative reinforcements, which can
come in the form of verbal reprimands, lowered grades, or
corporal punishment.

paradigm shift—A paradigm is a model or system that guides one's
thoughts about experiences. For example, an optimistic
person sees life with a paradigm that emphasizes the positive in situations. A paradigm shift occurs when a person
moves from one model to another.

performance assessment—Assessments or tests that have students
perform some authentic act such as writing, singing, or

playing a sport are performance assessments.

positive reinforcement—Rewards for valued behaviors are commonly called positive reinforcements. Higher grades, verbal praises, or candy given when a student offers a correct answer are all examples of positive reinforcement.

prescriptive grammar—Grammarians who attempt to preserve a certain set of language standards and who offer judgment on the relative correctness of language use are prescriptive grammarians.

primary documents—A text written for an authentic purpose. Having students read Henry David Thoreau's essays or the writings of Martin Luther King Jr. is exposing them to primary documents—as opposed to having them read someone else's explanation of Thoreau's or King's ideas.

prompt—A prompt is a statement that directs a student to perform a composition or a performance, generally for assessment. Most prompts provide the basic guidelines for the act, including topic, purpose, structure, and length.

reflection—As a teaching or learning tool, reflection is the act of thinking about one's actions or thoughts and providing a self-analysis of those acts or thoughts.

selected-response assessment—Assessments that require students to choose answers already provided on the test are selected-response assessments. Multiple-choice and matching exams are examples.

Standard English—The systems that guide the use of language include the cultural agreements that guide that usage. Standard English is the agreement the users of English have for forming and formatting language use.

standardized testing—Assessments that have standardized formats and purposes over large populations of test takers are often called standardized tests. These assessments are often highly regulated for validity and reliability.

stimulus/response—In behavioristic learning theory, the stimulus is the act, often by the teacher, that causes some response in the learner. In broad terms, if you touch the heated eye of a stove, the stimulus (the hot eye) causes you to jerk your hand away (response).

synoptic text—Texts written primarily to summarize large bodies of information. This is the most common type of textbook, typified by the high school history text.

theory of learning—Organized bodies of explanations for how people learn are generally called theories of learning. Behaviorism and constructivism are the primary competing theories of learning today.

usage—As a unique distinction from grammar, usage covers diction (word choice) and syntax (word order) in terms of how language is used within the confines of the grammar system.

writing forms—Typically, we discuss the genres of writing—what forms formal writing takes. Writing forms can be broken into two broad categories: prose and poetry. Prose is driven by sentence and paragraph formation, while poetry is driven by line and stanza formation. Another valuable distinction of form includes fiction versus nonfiction—whether the content is created (fiction) or primarily based in reality (nonfiction).

writing process—Traditionally, the writing process includes several components: prewriting, drafting, revising, editing, submitting, and publishing. The writing process does include these components, but they often occur in unique ways from writing to writer. Properly used, the term "writing process" should be a description of each writer's process instead of a template for others to follow.

writing workshops—A writing workshop is a classroom strategy and instruction process that allows class time for students to perform all the components of the writing process.

CHAPTER TWO

A History of Teaching Writing and a Synthesis of Research

Teaching writing as a field (the formal study of *how* to implement the field, such as the medical or the legal field) and writing as a content area (a body of knowledge worthy of study, such as biology or anthropology) has suffered a contentious and nebulous history; the teaching of writing has been both a long series of debates and a field hard to define clearly—along with being a relatively new field (Freedman et al., 1995). In fact, when the teaching of writing is examined throughout the twentieth century in classrooms from kindergarten through graduate school, we are more likely to find arguments about the teaching of grammar than to see the actual teaching of writing or students composing in those classrooms. Not only is the field nearly paralyzed by debate, but also it lacks a distinct character.

This chapter will examine the history of writing instruction by highlighting the perennial and current debates—the big questions—that influence and even inhibit effective and needed writing instruction by teachers and composing by our students. At the chapter's end, I will also outline the key concepts guiding effective writing instruction that have grown from bodies of research and the experiences of practitioners throughout the past century. The history and research of the field will help frame the implementation of a writing program in your classroom, the focus of Chapter Three.

As we creep deeper into the twenty-first century, ELA teachers are more and more likely to be familiar with leaders in the writing field such as Ralph Fletcher, George Hillocks, Constance Weaver, or Lucy Calkins; the National Writing Project (NWP) and the National Council of Teachers of English (NCTE) are also more influential than ever in classrooms across America. Yet, today the debates within the field of teaching writing differ little from those of the early- and mid-1900s during the career of Lou LaBrant— a prominent, though nearly forgotten, teacher of English who presided over NCTE in 1954 and influenced the field of ELA for nearly 50 years.

Tracing the career of LaBrant (Thomas, 2000a, 2001a) and referencing the work of contemporary leaders and research in the teaching of writing (Weaver, 1996; Hillocks, 1995; Zemelman, Daniels, & Hyde, 1998; NCTE's Writing Initiative), I will highlight the history of writing instruction throughout this chapter and raise key questions that must be addressed by any writing teacher before implementing a writing program that is effective and empowering. As I will show, today we need only to implement what we clearly have known about teaching writing for nearly seventy years or more. It is regrettable, but LaBrant's lament in 1947 is as true today as it was during the mid-twentieth century: "[A] considerable gap [exists] between the research currently available and the utilization of that research in school [writing] programs and methods" (p. 87).

Further, as I will address more closely in Chapter Five, writing instruction has garnered new and intense interest as a result of the National Assessment of Educational Progress' (NAEP) writing scores from 2002, the College Board's National Commission on

Writing in America's Schools and Colleges in 2003, and the revised SAT in 2005, along with the growing use of high-stakes tests in most states due to federal legislation, notably the legislation popularly referred to as No Child Left Behind. These external pressures merely intensify the debates that have existed throughout the past century. In most cases, the pressures have a negative impact on writing instruction; as they often increase a call to implement the least-effective practices for student improvement as writers and thinkers, the tests themselves become the goal of instruction at the expense of student composition.

The Cyclic Debates in the Teaching of Writing

When discussing educational debates, we have to be diligent not to fall victim to "either/or" thinking; much that we have to wrestle with in teaching and learning is far more complex than choosing between opposing stances. Often, the debate should not be reduced to *if* we should implement something, but *how* its implementation is most effective—and even *when* its implementation is effective. For the debates on teaching writing that we will consider in the following paragraphs, teachers must be mindful that we are searching for a proper perspective, a proper balance, a proper time for a variety of approaches that all contribute in some way to teaching students to write.

While the first chapter highlighted the concerns I have about assumptions driving the practice of teaching, I also attempted to suggest that we always consider and reconsider every stance we take to an educational problem. What we are seeking is the best approach at any one moment in the teaching-learning process. What I hope I am not implying is that one monolithic answer is at hand if only you would listen. I have no such delusion. The teaching of writing is a complex and ever-changing thing although some broad concepts can guide us well.

Many who unpack the traditional suitcase of writing instruction become falsely labeled as having no guidelines and no goals. LaBrant (1946), particularly in the middle of her career that spanned from 1906 until 1971, had to refute repeatedly "that [she was] advocating no correction, no emphasis on form" when promoting best practice in writing instruction by discounting the effectiveness of grammar workbook and textbook exercises that have historically dominated the instructional time allotted to writing instruction (p. 126). As we will see, the struggle for a writing teacher is not *if* she should foster grammatical correctness in student compositions, but *how* to do so within the context of the larger goal—students becoming independent and thoughtful writers.

As mentioned above, the external pressure to address writing is high today, but it is nothing new; LaBrant (1959) felt the pressure herself: "Suddenly the public believes we have not taught . . . writing well enough" (p. 299). Our standards mania is nothing new either. LaBrant (1952a) wrestled with, "Is it possible to teach a changing population a changing language and still give them something they can use, something they can cherish—standards, if you will?" (p. 346). Under the weight of public scrutiny and the call for high standards, ELA teachers then and now have to face the following questions.

What are the roles of grammar instruction and student composition in the teaching of writing? This is possibly the single greatest problem teachers of writing face. Leaders in the field of writing instruction (Weaver, 1996; Hillocks, 1995; Zemelman, Daniels, & Hyde, 1998) are clear about the appropriate weight given to grammar instruction (I will use the term "grammar" broadly throughout this discussion to include issues of Standard English and conventions of grammar, mechanics, and usage in the writing of English) and students composing original works of writing. They are also clear about the *how* and the *when*. The end of this chapter will summarize that research on writing instruction.

A first explanation concerning the history of writing instruction is that students have been taught grammar in isolated and worksheet-bound ways far too often, at the expense of any significant time being spent in class with students actually composing original works and following those compositions through several drafts that include attention to **revision** strategies addressing the content, style, and form of that writing. In most ELA classes, even when students have written essays a disproportionate amount of time and energy is spent on the **surface features** of the writing—with teachers focusing primarily on students **editing** the grammar, mechanics, and usage so that the writing conforms to Standard English.

Throughout her career, LaBrant identified the failure to implement research on writing instruction in the classroom and to foster effective writers through **isolated grammar instruction**. In 1946, she identified "hundreds of studies" that revealed little or no transfer of grammar skills from direct grammar instruction to student compositions, supporting her advocacy for having students write instead of completing grammar worksheets (p. 127). Additionally, two statements from LaBrant serve our discussion well here: "Knowing *about* writing and its parts does not bring it about, just as owning a blueprint does not give you a house" (LaBrant, 1957, p. 256) and "I am not willing to teach the polishing and adornment of irresponsible, unimportant writing" (LaBrant, 1946, p. 123). During her own schooling and her life as an English teacher and teacher of English teachers, LaBrant watched as teachers placed a greater importance on isolated grammatical knowledge than on the implementation of grammatical skills within original and effective student writings.

In this first question, we have ample evidence from researchers and practitioners that the following guidelines are most effective when our goal is to foster written composition skills in our students.

- Students learn to write by writing; their development is aided by having choice both in the content and the form those works take.
- Students need direct grammar, mechanics, and usage instruction based on their written performances, preferably targeted at the areas demonstrated in that writing. Whole-class, iso-

revision

The act of reconsidering a draft of writing and changing or expanding elements of that draft for a final version.

surface features

The combined elements of grammar, usage, and mechanics are called surface features, as they are all addressed in editing during revision.

editing

Identifying surface-feature conformity to Standard English in a final draft.

isolated grammar instruction

The direct instruction of grammar, usage, and mechanics through workbook or textbook exercises.

lated direct grammar instruction may improve grammatical knowledge in students, but it clearly does not improve the surface features of students' original writing—and it may in fact negatively impact that writing (Weaver, 1996; Hillocks, 1995; Zemelman, Daniels, & Hyde, 1998).

■ To develop composition skills in students, fluency (the willingness to write) should be more heavily emphasized for the youngest writers; the emphasis on conventions and correctness should be gradually emphasized as the student matures but never at the expense of fluency or the content of the student's composition. Weaver (1996) believes we have to move students through three levels of concern without destroying the earlier levels—from **fluency** to **clarity** to correctness.

■ Writing instruction and assessment must reflect that the content of student writing is of greatest value, while maintaining for the student an understanding that ultimately surface features impact directly on that meaning.

fluency
A person's willingness and eagerness to produce writing.

clarity
In writing, the point or points must be clear at both the grammatical and content levels.

LaBrant clearly placed her instructional emphasis on the quality of the ideas and the expression in student writing; she also regretted "the fear of writing" in students that resulted from "a continuance of too early and too rigid demands" placed by teachers on surface features (LaBrant, 1952b, p. 128). Essentially, LaBrant noted that ELA teachers "seem[ed] to resent or refuse to recognize change" (1952a, p. 341), and students were left to "[do] everything but the writing of many complete papers" (1953, p. 417). This assessment is characteristic of the history of writing instruction in ELA classrooms, and far too often today the same claim can be made.

As early as 1934, LaBrant saw that "when the child writes or speaks of an experience which has become clear, he can manage the construction" (p. 64)—recognizing the direct link between meaning and surface features in student compositions. In other words, grammar errors in student writing may often be a reflection of unclear thought, a lack of student interest in an assigned topic, or many things other than a lack of student expertise in language. If we as ELA teachers look critically at our experiences, we see that many years of direct instruction of surface features have had little impact on how well students conform to Standard English in their writing; instead of asking for more of the same, we might investigate why such a disconnect exists. This leads to the second question and the issue of writing forms and student choice.

What form should student writing take? Possibly the one constant in writing instruction throughout the past 100 years has been the tendency to assign students the traditional essay as the central part of a writing program, with the occasional short fiction or poetry assignment thrown in as a lesser assignment. LaBrant (1934) recognized early in her career "a large gap between natural expression and the stilted performance which passes as a school composition" (p. 62). In effect, she saw the traditional essay assigned to students for what it is—artificial.

In the first half of the twentieth century, the traditional five-paragraph essay—with an introduction including a thesis establishing three points, three body paragraphs developing those three points, and a conclusion repeating the focus of the paper—became the goal of writing instruction in American schools. During the last fifty years, that rigidity has lessened some, but the essay still dominates the central focus of classroom assignments in its original form and its hybrids; in fact, under the weight of high-stakes testing, the five-paragraph essay has made a significant and damaging resurgence (Hillocks, 2003). As we will discuss further in the following chapters, this template approach to teaching writing must be abandoned entirely for authentic writing forms.

With my discussion from Chapter One in mind, you may be able to see that the artificial nature of the traditional essay has more to do with the assumptions about learning than it does with authentic writing. It *seems* logical to reduce writing to a template to help the novice writer, but as we will discuss, that assumption is false. Remember that most of our students want to *see* what the assembled bicycle looks like; only a small percentage of students want step-by-step directions.

Beyond confronting traditional essay forms, LaBrant challenged the standard definition for "creative writing" as well, which had been limited to fiction, poetry, and drama. LaBrant (1936) preferred to label writing "creative" when "the writer has determined his own subject, the form in which he presents it, and the length of the product" (p. 293). LaBrant confronted and redefined the assumptions of our field in order to reshape her instruction and help students become real writers. In contrast to current assumptions about essay and writing assignments in classrooms that have been prevalent throughout the history of our schools, these guidelines are essential to effective writing programs.

- Writing instruction should support and allow student choice in the content of their writing. As often as possible, teachers must allow students to choose the topics of their writing assignments. In one sense, this adds rigor to the assignment since that choice becomes part of the student performance. Additionally, the very fact that students have choice helps support ownership and empowerment by the student.

- Writing instruction should support and allow student choice in the form of their writing. As with content choice, the choice of form adds rigor and increases engagement. An element of constructivist learning theory that many fail to acknowledge is that it encourages teachers to shift the burden of learning to the learner, which facilitates more authentic understanding by those learners.

- Guided and prompt-driven writing assignments and instruction are *essential* as well but should be used proportionately less often than writing assignments and instruction driven by student choice and should be implemented in support of these larger writing assignments. When teachers use prompts for writing, those prompts should support clear teaching goals. Based on student writing samples, teachers might see a need for addressing sentence variety; in this case a prompt prescribing sentence variety would be completely appropriate.

- Writing teachers should recognize that all writing driven by student choices is "creative" in that it is original, and that all writing, regardless of genre, requires a great deal of skill in diction, syntax, and style by the writer. This includes manipulating literary and rhetorical techniques that have been traditionally limited to discussions of fiction and poetry.

- Writing teachers should avoid template approaches to writing assignments that teach students a writing form that essentially exists only in classroom assignments; the form that original pieces of writing take is an act of discovery and an issue of appropriateness, but there is no template for an authentic piece of writing. One caveat with this guideline is that there are high-stakes testing situations that value template writing. When teachers and students are faced with standardized writing assessments that require certain template approaches to writing, teachers should teach that as one type of writing—what we might call a "test-writing" genre. What we must guard against is allowing this one inauthentic form to *become* the writing program because the stakes of the test are so high.

For many decades, from the 1920s into the early 1970s, LaBrant offered an example for bringing authentic writing to the classroom, yet, over the past decades and even today, inauthentic forms of essay writing have dominated our classroom writing programs. As I will explore in greater detail in Chapter Three, students should have access to all the *freedoms* and *responsibilities* of published writers, of composing authentic works, just as art students paint and draw on empty canvases.

Should writing assignments vary depending on the ability level of the student? Historically, American schools have been stratified, particularly in language instruction; students are usually grouped with peers sharing similar literacy abilities. The Blue Birds (the top group) and Buzzards (the weak students) reading groups that are often referred to in jest are real parts of the history of reading instruction—and real parts of the current practices in reading instruction. Students being taught and assessed differently by their perceived abilities is also common in writing instruction. For LaBrant (1950), the guiding principle, "that *doing* careful writing is the best device for *understanding* careful writing," stood for all children: "You may say this is the opportunity for the gifted only. I do not think so" (pp. 187, 188).

At any point over the past one hundred years, we are more apt to find weaker students completing worksheets and receiving direct and isolated grammar instruction while the perceived stronger students have greater opportunities to write. Additionally, those students labeled weaker are also more likely to have less-experienced and weaker teachers than the more accomplished students. The writing program I will explain in the following chapter will refute that hidden tradition; for writing instruction, all students need the same essential program based on writing driven by choice in form and content.

Sameness is something we should neither strive for nor expect in others. We must, however, engage our students in similarly rich linguistic experiences. From those experiences, we will read a wide range of products from our writing students, and we should expect and embrace this range.

What attitude should teachers have toward errors in Standard English and in students' ideas? The teaching of ELA has been characterized by a fairly rigid attitude of prescription and a value placed on linguistic correctness. "We have spent years teaching platitudes about sincerity in composition, sincerity in literature," noted LaBrant (1936), yet "we have defeated our teaching by telling students what to say and how to say it" (p. 298). The prescriptive mentality failed in many ways, she believed; for our discussion here, the teacher's attitude toward correctness is central to either fostering or destroying a writing program that produces independent writers and empowered students. LaBrant (1943) recognized that "prejudices and snobberies" about language often ruined any effectiveness in instruction, particularly in writing. "We must be careful in criticizing the writing of the young. . . . [We] should not under the guise of developing literary standards, merely pass along adult weariness," she added (1949, pp. 275–276).

As I will show at the end of the chapter, ELA teachers must shift their attitudes away from prescriptive attitudes about language to more descriptive, and thus more authentic, ones. The perception that language is frozen and driven by rules is inaccurate, and it directly inhibits fluency in student writing. Reframing one's attitude towards grammar and usage, particularly in light of the history of the English language and the development of the "rules" of Standard English, will dramatically change the effectiveness of writing instruction (Williams 1990).

Can a teacher of writing be effective without being a writer? No. "The teacher should know the agony of putting words on paper [since] . . . [w]riting is hard work," LaBrant (1955, p. 71)) believed. I would add that teachers need to be practicing writers who write with a purpose—preferably submitting work for publication. Writing, like the visual arts, playing a musical instrument, or playing a sport, is a performance; in schools, virtually all of the people in charge of those activities have practiced and continue to practice in their fields. In higher education, a student in chemistry class is more often than not being taught by a practicing chemist. If we can change our perception of what our purposes are as teachers, then we can begin to shift our goals from transferring a validated body of knowledge (consider Freire's banking concept of education) from an authority (the teacher) to the student, to fostering within students an understanding of the processes at the core of the fields being studied. Within that shift is a need for teachers to be experts, as well as practitioners, in their fields, yet the sad fact of ELA teaching is that those teachers are rarely practicing writers at any level. One avenue to changing that situation is the work of the National Writing Project, which supports local affiliates that provide summer institutes designed to teach teachers to be writers and thus better writing teachers. I will deal more with this in Chapter Five.

The five broad questions dealt with above are not exhaustive of the field of teaching writing, but I believe they capture the tensions that exist now—and have persisted throughout the greater part of modern American education. These tensions characterize the field and point to why writing instruction is often less than effective. Some of these issues are more recent, such as the writing process; therefore, the final section of this chapter will synthesize and summarize the bodies of research we currently have concerning the teaching of writing.

Research on the Teaching of Writing—A Synthesis

Before I outline the major research findings concerning writing instruction, I need to offer a few warnings about this research. First, I will be offering the evidence from *bodies* of research (although I will follow the common practice of referring to individual studies that are reflective of those bodies of research); often we respond far too quickly and carelessly to single studies. Writing has decades and decades of research revealing tendencies that can be implemented with a fair amount of certainty that these strategies will be effective.

I will also be dealing with what research says about effective practices for producing student writers; if we change the goal of instruction, the findings below would change as well. Simply put, if a teacher's goal is to create a grammarian, then direct and isolated grammar instruction becomes an effective strategy, but if a teacher's goal is to foster writers, then actual student writing must drive the instruction.

Further, I should add that the research findings summarized below are best implemented in settings that embrace constructivist learning theory and

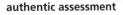

authentic assessment

Assessments that reflect as nearly as possible acts and performances found in the world outside of school .

practice **authentic assessment**. When those parameters are changed, the effectiveness of each strategy discussed is impacted. This summary is drawn primarily from the works of Weaver (1996), Hillocks (1995), Williams (1990), Pinker (1994), NCTE's Writing Initiative information (provided on their web site: www.ncte.org), the extensive work of the National Center for the Study of Writing (its research is available at NWP's web site, www.writingproject.org) and Zemelman, Daniels, and Hyde (1998).

The major concepts found in the research on writing instruction are as follows:

- Students of all ages have pre-wired linguistic abilities, including grammatical systems (Pinker, 1994); they also come to school with a background in language that may support or hinder their writing performances (NCTE). Writing programs must value that humans' natural linguistic abilities *and* the linguistic environment of all students deeply impacts their writing abilities at any point in their education. A student's ability to write is a product of both nature and nurture.

- Writing ability in students is enhanced by literacy and other so-called "creative" activities such as drawing (Weaver, 1996; NCTE). Holistic approaches to literacy must support a writing program; writing by its nature is a creative act, so a writing program benefits from additional creative activities such as visual art or music.

- Writing is best performed in a group setting, including student-teacher interactions in conferences and peer editing (Hillocks, 1995; NCTE). Learning is rarely best achieved as a solitary act; a democratic society should encourage learning within a group setting. Writing requires a great deal of individual effort; therefore, a student benefits greatly from having opportunities to work on writing with peers and groups. Part of the writing process should include the formation of drafts and interaction among several readers, both teachers and peers. One misconception that plagues the proper use of peer editing is the fear of cheating. We must insure that students learn to distinguish between the sharing of ideas and cheating.

- Student writing is enhanced by student choice and engagement in the content and form of their writing (Hillocks, 1995; NCTE). All learning improves when the learner is engaged. That engagement is best fostered through autonomy, by allowing students a choice in what they write about and how they express their ideas. A cycle of learning, engagement, and choice helps create a classroom where students are intrinsically motivated, where they write to see a finished piece and not to receive a grade.

- Writing is best learned by writing often, in a variety of genres while also reading a variety of genres (NCTE). Talk to any sports coach; players love to scrimmage. For the athlete, virtually nothing can top a game. Writing is both the instructional strategy and the goal as with a sport. Just as a coach guides players during a scrimmage so the players can see the concepts in action, a writing teacher needs to coach students as they write.

- Direct and isolated grammar, mechanics, and usage instruction does not enhance student writing quality (Weaver, 1996; NCTE) but has been found to negatively impact the quality of student writing (Hillocks, 1995). As with the point above, when a coach turns all practices into drills—or if a coach turned all sports teams into practice teams with no matches played!—the authenticity is lost and engagement is nullified. Once again, if our goal is to create student writers, we have to eliminate "skill-and-drill," where the students practice isolated and inauthentic skills in worksheet or text exercise formats only to be tested in the same isolated manner.

- Direct *writing* instruction, however, is necessary and effective when embedded within having students write by choice and when that direct instruction supports those larger writing assignments (Ray and Laminack, 2001; Weaver, 1996).

Though we are refuting the value of direct grammar instruction, we are not discounting direct instruction. As I will discuss in Chapter Three, some teacher-driven writing exercises are needed and effective.

- The best assessment of a student's writing ability is the assessment of actual student compositions—not selected-response assessments of isolated language skills (NCTE; Popham, 2003). Too many experts in the field of assessment have spent decades attempting to correlate selected-response assessment (which is quick, cheap, and easy) with authentic assessment in order to justify objective tests. The practice may be easily supported by numbers, but we can never allow conclusions to be made about students as writers on anything other than original compositions by those students. I will touch on this later, but we must add that those assessments must always be done by humans—not computers.

rubrics

Detail the characteristics that correlate for each level of proficiency in a task.

- **Rubrics** to guide writing instruction and writing assessment can provide valuable support for writing instruction, but, carelessly implemented, they can actually negatively impact writing instruction (Popham, 2003; Mabry, 1999; Hillocks, 2003; Ray and Laminack, 2001). All rubrics are not created equal. Rubrics used to guide student performances and assist teachers in assessing work are effective *only* if they avoid being a template for those performances. Effective rubrics remain at the conceptual level, allowing for a range of performances as well as the expert judgment of teachers in the final assessment of their students' work. Asking students to participate in the creation of a rubric for a writing assignment may be a more useful strategy than actually using that rubric, since it would lead to a discussion of the concepts that guide effective writing and would expose the never-ending debates of the field of writing to students.

- Student writing improves when teacher feedback on that writing requires specific and meaningful actions by the student (Reeves, 2004).

The tradition in responding to student writing is rich in red marks on a student essay. We saw a period when teachers were admonished for excessively marking their students' writing; some even called for an end to marking student work. What we never fully embraced is the need to respond to student writing—yes, to mark on student drafts—but to do so with the type of targeted comments that give students something to do when they revise. One quality of our comments is that we should ask questions—"Why did you begin the piece about your grandfather without ever mentioning his name?" This sort of question helps push a student writer to understand the value in details. Another quality of our comments should be to help students develop revision strategies. In my own writing system, I label all my comments on students' writing with one of three suggested actions—edit, delete, or add. These revision approaches guide students with something to do when they revise.

- Teachers who write and are professional writers offer effective writing instruction (NCTE; Ray and Laminack, 2001). Unlike the classic analogy found on the SAT of old, writing exists in our real world for all to see. The writing classroom needs to be a place rich in the works of professional writers, and students need to be in daily contact with someone who struggles with writing—their teacher.

- Instruction in the transmission mode (what commonly would be called lecturing) as the dominant instructional method is ineffective for writing instruction; instruction that balances student needs and interests (student centered), targeted direct instruction by the teacher (teacher centered), and clearly defined learning tasks (performance centered) is most effective. Instruction that allows students to learn naturally has proven to be moderately effective as have student-teacher writing conferences (Hillocks, 1995). Forty or even thirty years ago, we did not have the body of evidence we have today, but we now have a growing body of research on what creates valuable writing by students. As writing teachers we should know this research and practice these strategies while always seeking a richer understanding of what works best.

- Student writing quality has been shown to be negatively impacted by isolated grammar instruction; however, inquiry activities, rubric-based writing instruction, sentence combining, and writing from models have all proven to be effective (Hillocks, 1995; Weaver, 1996). Many writing researchers have documented a wide range of direct instruction that supports student writing. I am not advocating that teachers simply quit teaching but am rather suggesting that many of our efforts are not actually addressing writing.

- A descriptive attitude toward grammar, mechanics, and usage is more conducive to writing instruction than a prescriptive attitude (Williams, 1990; Weaver, 1996). For an effective writing workshop atmosphere, many teachers (myself included) have found that portraying the ever-evolving nature of language supports our goal of students as writers better than an emphasis on error and correctness. Again, this does not mean that we discount Standard English; it is a matter of *how*, not *if*.

anchor papers

Sample essays offered as examples of each score assigned to essays on standardized tests of writing.

- High-stakes testing of writing, along with test-endorsed rubrics and **anchor papers** (the sample papers offered as examples of each score), negatively impacts writing instruction and thus the quality of student writing (Hillocks, 2003; Mabry, 1999; Freedman, 1995). The high-stakes testing movement and the influx of computer-graded writing are certain to increase some of the worst practices in writing instruction. While we must adequately prepare our students for such assessments, I have to re-emphasize that we should not allow such a concern to become our writing program.

These research findings will form the basis for the discussion that follows in Chapter Three concerning the bringing of effective writing instruction into the classroom. What teachers of writing must also understand, though, is that the daily teaching of writing is as varied as each student we meet. In other words, although the research may support broad practices and refute this or that instructional practice, we may occasionally swim against the research because the student or the moment calls for such a change. It is likely, for example, that some students may actually blossom as writers when provided with very structured writing forms and assignments that are directed by the teacher; others may be empowered, engaged, and inspired by the direct study of grammar.

Research, whether it concerns writing instruction or other aspects of education, should never be seen as demonizing anything; at the same time, it should never be seen as endorsing any strategy. In the teaching of writing, we must not cast anything aside, and we must remain critical of even the most well-supported strategies. If one truism exists, it is that the teaching of writing is an organic field—growing, and thus always in flux.

Reconsidering the Discussion So Far

Throughout Chapter Two, I have moved us into seeing, broadly, the history of the field of teaching writing, and into the fairly recent growth of solid research on effective writing instruction. As I did in Chapter One, I want to end this chapter with a cautionary note.

We should look critically and closely at the history of teaching writing, and we should know the research on that field as it now stands. But beyond those simple acts of knowing, we must become active both in the history now being made and the research yet to be considered. Let's then consider a few questions once again:

- What have been the guiding reasons behind our instructional strategies as writing teachers over the past hundred years? How effective have those practices been? What goal or standard should that assessment be measured against?

- Historically, which students have been left outside the field of writing? Why? Has that trend changed? If not, how can it be changed?
- What areas of writing instruction have been well covered by research? What areas have been ignored?
- What political baggage comes with writing instruction? Is it the same as with reading? Why or why not?

The writing field is still young and vibrant enough that we as practitioners can make a difference. With that in mind, we have to know where we have been and must know where we are going.

Chapter Three will now turn to the classroom. I will put flesh on the bones of the discussion so far. From theory, history, and research, we will move to writing instruction in the classroom—where things matter most.

Glossary

anchor papers—Sample essays offered as examples of each score assigned to essays on standardized tests of writing are often called the anchor papers, as they serve as a reference for those scoring the tests.

authentic assessment—Assessments that reflect as nearly as possible acts and performances found in the world outside of school are authentic assessments. In athletics, athletic performance is judged on match day—the success reflected in the outcome of an actual match. For art students, we tend to look at a work of art or a portfolio of works. These are authentic in assessing the performance in its totality as it would be enacted outside of a school or assessment situation. Nowhere in the real world do we take multiple-choice tests; they are only a thing of schooling, and are thus inauthentic.

clarity—In writing, the point or points must be clear at both the grammatical and content levels.

editing—Identifying surface-feature conformity to Standard English in a final draft of composing. Editing deals primarily with surface features and is one aspect of the larger concept of revision.

fluency—In writing, fluency refers to a person's willingness and eagerness to produce writing. Many believe that fluency must be fostered first, and must be protected throughout a person's development as a writer.

isolated grammar instruction—The direct instruction of grammar, usage, and mechanics through workbook or textbook exercises. The lessons are taught outside of the context of students' own writing and primarily with the learning of grammar standards as the goal.

revision—The act of reconsidering a draft of writing and changing or expanding elements of that draft for a final version. Editing is simply one element of revision, and the two should not be used interchangeably.

rubrics—Often used to guide student performances and to identify assessment guidelines, a rubric details the characteristics that correlate for each level of proficiency in a task. Many states provide a simple rubric for grading student essays holistically. The College Board offers rubrics for the written sections of both [sd9]Advanced Placement tests in English.

surface features—The combined elements of grammar, usage, and mechanics are called surface features, as they are all addressed in editing during revision.

CHAPTER THREE

Teaching Writing— In the Classroom

"You can't teach people to write well. Writing well is something God lets you do or declines to let you do"—thus claims Kurt Vonnegut (1974), much to the dismay of those of us who believe we *can* teach our students to write (p. 25). Vonnegut is right, in a way; the teaching of writing is itself an abusrdity. We cannot *directly* teach our students to write, but we certainly can *foster* wonderful writers. That will be the focus of this chapter—how to implement the teaching of writing in actual classrooms with the greatest effectiveness.

The discussion that follows will deal with the following areas: the expertise, roles, and attitudes of the teacher; the characteristics and implementation of a writing program; the day-to-day issues of teaching writing; the instructional concerns and the roles of students when teaching writing; and implementing direct instruction in all aspects of writing instruction. As I begin this introduction to teaching writing as it looks in the classroom on a daily basis, I want to add that offering this picture does not suggest that a template exists for teaching writing, just as a template for a dynamic piece of writing does not exist. While I will offer specifics and examples, I caution that I do not mean to imply a script—only a series of concepts that will serve teachers of writing well as they wrestle with each student they encounter.

The Writing Teacher—"The Most Intimate of All Teaching"

"Teaching English is probably the most intimate of all teaching," proclaimed LaBrant (1964, p. 34). The teaching of literacy is a uniquely human endeavor—a discourse between and among people about the most defining act that makes us human, our ability to communicate through language. This brings us to another paradox: while writing is best taught in a student-centered environment, the expertise, personality, and decision-making abilities of the teacher are essential to the success of that instruction. The teacher must be the dominant expert in the room while simultaneously attempting to be invisible, guarding against being imposing, and eventually rendering herself useless.

John Gardner (1999) begins his *On Becoming a Novelist* by asking the reader to consider the qualities that seem to be typical of novelists—their temperament, their habits, their drive; his discussion as a practicing writer of those qualities is a wonderful glimpse into the writer and the writer's life. I believe such a consideration is valuable for us here as we explore what qualities seem to be present in the most effective writing teachers. These qualities are not intended to be exhaustive, and I feel that these are not *intrinsically* innate qualities. In other words, most of these qualities can be goals as much as markers for teachers of writing who hope to grow as writing teachers and professionals.

While Kohn's *Beyond Discipline* (1996) is a text on classroom management, he advances a premise about a teacher's attitude toward children and toward using coercion to achieve compliance from students

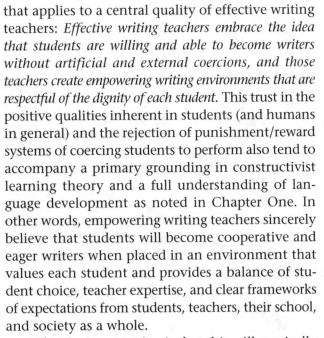

that applies to a central quality of effective writing teachers: *Effective writing teachers embrace the idea that students are willing and able to become writers without artificial and external coercions, and those teachers create empowering writing environments that are respectful of the dignity of each student.* This trust in the positive qualities inherent in students (and humans in general) and the rejection of punishment/reward systems of coercing students to perform also tend to accompany a primary grounding in constructivist learning theory and a full understanding of language development as noted in Chapter One. In other words, empowering writing teachers sincerely believe that students will become cooperative and eager writers when placed in an environment that values each student and provides a balance of student choice, teacher expertise, and clear frameworks of expectations from students, teachers, their school, and society as a whole.

What I am not saying is that this will magically or even quickly occur. Students can become willing and eager writers, but many reach your classrooms as neither. The culture and practices of all the cumulative classrooms before yours are the foundations upon which those students form their expectations of you, your classroom, and writing in general. Creating the writing classroom I am encouraging is often a long and arduous transition for the students, one that must be carefully monitored by the teacher.

The drive to fill students' minds with proper grammar, correct their many linguistic flaws, and coerce them to comply with the dictates of good literature is common in ELA classrooms (again, a fault of the banking concept of education refuted by Freire), but it fails in the teaching of writing. This leads us to a second characteristic of effective writing teachers: *Effective writing teachers embrace a descriptive stance concerning what makes writing effective, what constitutes Standard English, and what defines outstanding literature.* This descriptive perspective reflects an awareness that standards are organic and relative (to both people and time); in other words, they are constantly in a state of flux—although some broad qualities do hold true at any moment. (The Elizabethans clearly had standards for language and literature just as we do in contemporary America though the two sets of standards differ.) The essential qualities that make writing effective and engaging must be part of the expertise of the writing teacher, yet they are qualities that are always being reconsidered and brought to life by that teacher and are ultimately left for all students to discover on their own by being immersed in literature, language, and the writer's life. It is the teacher's job to offer opportunities for students to see those same qualities (not through acts of coercion) and to take an ever-evolving attitude toward language, literature, and writing.

How, then, does an effective writing teacher have high standards for students? How does an effective writing teacher judge, evaluate, and even categorize the writings of students within these first two characteristics that seem to refute any judgment? This is a serious and difficult problem. Writing teachers owe students both a respect for the dignity of their humanity and an honest and authentic evaluation of their works within the context of the standards of the field and society at large. *Effective writing teachers balance a respect for students, a professional and complex representation of the field of writing, and a clear and sincere portrayal of the expectations within the field and society.* The teacher needs to find instructional strategies and learning opportunities that foster an awareness within students of their own writing standards, an awareness of the criteria used to evaluate student writing both within the ELA class and in other classes throughout the school, and an awareness of the assessment criteria and social expectations that will be imposed on them by standardized tests and in their lives beyond the walls of the classroom. Achieving this balancing act is one of the most challenging aspects of teaching writing, but it is also one of the most rewarding. More on how this looks in the classroom will follow in this chapter and in Chapter Four.

The teacher's expertise about writing, while difficult to separate from any of the qualities discussed above, is ultimately central to his effectiveness as a writing teacher. That expertise must be seen as always evolving; one cannot simply learn what makes writing great (and how to teach that) and be done with it. The education of the writing teacher, like the education of the writer, is never finished: *Effective writing teachers live inductive lives as readers (who read like writers) and as writers, filling their lives and the lives of their students with a wide variety of classic and contemporary works of writing in all genres.* A common scenario in an engaging writing classroom might include a teacher explaining to her students that she had just read a piece by a writer new to her which completely changed how she viewed the written word. An effective writing teacher has a somewhat childlike wonderment about language and literature that is in great contrast to the staid attitude, often associated with ELA teachers, of being concerned mostly with protecting the rules, preserving the canon, and correcting their students.

This brings us to our final quality: *Effective writing teachers live the writer's life; they are writers themselves, both by choice in their professional lives and as models within their classrooms.* Though I will elaborate further on this in Chapter Five, it cannot be stressed enough: very few things will enhance the quality of writing instruction more than the teacher's own engagement with writing.

The intimacy of helping another person grow as a writer has always unnerved me. It is an act that forces me to grow and to change. While the five qualities I have described above are broadly defined and certainly not exhaustive, I believe they offer useful reference points for the effective writing teacher's own growth and change. Now all the effective writing teacher needs is an effective writing program. (A helpful outline of how best to prepare teachers of writing can be found at the NCTE home page: www.ncte.org/about/over/positions/level/coll/107683.htm.)

Implementing a Writing Program:
The Writing Workshop

"For the writing workshop to be successful," Katie Wood Ray (Ray and Laminack, 2001) explains, "it must be highly structured and must work the same way basically every day so that it could almost run itself independent of directed activity" (pp. 14–15). Along with Atwell (1998) and Calkins (1994), Ray speaks for the researchers and practitioners who support the writing workshop as the unifying concept for implementing a writing program. Many who have lived the traditional, grammar-driven history of writing instruction tend to mischaracterize authentic writing instruction as lacking structure, standards, or direct instruction. In fact, says Ray, "the writing workshop is a highly structured place" (p. 14). At the same time, it is an extremely adaptable space, as varied as the students who come to learn and write within it. An effective writing teacher must come to see that a class valuing student choice and individual freedom is *not* in contrast with a need for structure.

Let's start our discussion here with a slightly different area for initial comparison. When teachers of reading are asked how they teach reading, they often reply with something such as, "We use the Willy-Nilly Reading Program." In other words, many classroom teachers come to think in terms of commercial programs at the expense of the guiding concepts of a field. That said, I believe the key to teaching writing well is to implement a cohesive writing program within your classroom. Ideally, this will be part of a school-wide program, driven by broad but unifying concepts of best practice regardless of the teachers, students, or materials (commercial or teacher made) involved.

Whether you are teaching beginning literacy to primary students, dealing with integrated ELA skills within several content areas at the middle levels, teaching the traditional survey English classes at the high school, or addressing composition directly at the college level, you must begin by clarifying for yourself where the teaching of writing fits within any equal or larger instructional goals. This context will shape the decisions made concerning all the remaining aspects of a writing program that we will explore here.

The best unifying metaphor for a writing program is the workshop, since it implies direct practice of the field and a certain level of structure combined with the open-ended nature of independent projects. But how does the workshop look? And how can a teacher operating under the highly directed, hierarchical demands of most classrooms implement something as individualized as a writing workshop?

We'll begin this description of the writing workshop by addressing the misconceptions highlighted by Ray. The writing workshop is *not* a freewheeling, feel-good playtime for students to do as they please while the teacher sits idly by. It *is* a place where everyone writes with purpose and by choice (including the teacher), and where the teacher, *driven by the evidence of what students compose,* offers directed lessons and specific feedback that shape the growth of both the workshop and each student as a writer.

Ray and Laminack (2001), Atwell (1998), and Calkins (1994) offer qualities and characteristics that tend to mark effective writing workshops, including the following points.

- The students and teachers within a writing workshop are dedicated to daily writing with purpose and to recreating as vividly as possible the writing life within the classroom. Teachers who implement a writing workshop within a required course (as opposed to an elected course where we will assume students are already engaged by choosing the class) will implement strategies to gain the authentic engagement of each student in this main goal.

- Many, if not all, of the major writing assignments that students complete through all the stages of the writing process are governed by writer choice in both content and form. While we will place a premium on choice in student writing, we must not feel bound to any *one* approach to the assignment of writing. Choice is essential and should be prevalent, but something nearly as important is that our students have a variety of purposes and guides for their writing. Regardless of our quest for authenticity, school still remains school, and thus (to a certain degree) artificial.

■ The writing workshop offers student writers regular, large blocks of time for writing in all the stages of the writing process. The workshop also offers students time to work alone, with a peer, in groups, and with the teacher (and occasionally with an expert writer brought in from outside the school).

■ The writing workshop is filled with a wide variety of authentic texts in the form of classic and contemporary writers, in all genres, and at the disposal of all students by choice and when guided. Again, reading choice is crucial, but so is variety. The writing workshop provides many books by many writers from many times and backgrounds. And students are encouraged to read often and widely.

■ The workshop is punctuated with direct teaching that I will often refer to as "**mini-lessons**" (in the sense used by Atwell and others). This instructional approach usually grows from needs revealed in students' own writing *and* from the expertise of the writing teacher. Mini-lessons are brief (maybe ten to fifteen minutes long) and deal with direct writing instruction, **craft lessons**, author studies, literature studies, or a wide variety of student needs or course requirements.

■ Writing workshops are often noisy. While the physical set-up of the classroom must provide for students who have differing needs to compose (are places available for students who need a quiet space to write?), the effective writing teacher embraces the need for productive talk that grows from a piece of literature, a mini-lesson, a writing conference, a writing exercise, or simply a strategy to get the linguistic motors running. Writing workshops allow and encourage students to talk as a natural and essential part of the writing process.

---

mini-lessons

Lessons of about ten to fifteen minutes that are planned and directed by the teacher. This concept is often associated with Atwell (1998); the teacher uses a brief lesson as punctuated and directed lessons within the context of a workshop where students are highly active.

---

craft lesson

Lessons that deal with a writer's use of purposeful techniques. A writer's craft includes literary technique, diction, syntax, and style along with virtually any strategy that writers use to manipulate and control meaning.

I would like to make some distinctions here that we often fail to make with students. We should clarify four situations for students concerning talk and silence in the classroom—productive talk, non-productive talk, engaged silence, and disengaged silence. In a writing workshop, we want to help foster productive talk and engaged silence while avoiding non-productive talk and disengaged silence (though I would argue that the last two situations dominate our classrooms because of the discipline battles we create).

writing exercises
Brief assigned writing by students that have an instructional purpose other than a finished writing piece. They often have highly directed guidelines or prompts, and they may spring from teacher expertise, curriculum guidelines, or student needs.

- Writing workshops are punctuated by **writing exercises** along with writing compositions. Writing exercises are often prompted (directions, content guidelines, and form guidelines are provided), teacher driven (though the teacher is best served by working from demonstrated student needs and her own expertise in writing), and not intended to require students to follow through in all areas of the writing process. (I will offer some writing exercises at the end of this chapter on the discussion of direct instruction—though many valuable resources exist, including Gardner [1991].)

- Writing workshops have authentic publishing goals for students within the classroom, within the school, and through outside publications. Submitting original works for publication must accompany the assessment of writing by the teacher if a writing workshop is to remain authentic.

- Writing workshops strive to balance the humanity of each student (who happens often to be in the frustrating position of being a novice) with the rigor and standards of the field of writing. Students must feel safe to experiment and to fail without fear of punishment (especially in the form of lower grades), but they must also become aware of the criteria by which all writers are judged in the larger community. Teachers must work constantly to maintain fluency in student writers, while simultaneously moving those students toward a state of clarity and an awareness of conventions, along with an ability to apply those conventions by choice and with purpose.

- Writing workshops have systems and procedures (such as Nancie Atwell's in her *In the Middle* [1998]), but the systems and procedures themselves can be as varied as the teachers. Without systems and procedures, students often fail to achieve under the weight of *managing* their writing while trying to become writers. Most teachers benefit from beginning with someone else's management structures before adapting a system to their proclivities and to the needs of their students.

- Writing workshops provide the essential tools for composing, which include the means of writing (pen, pencil, etc.), paper, writer's journals, word processing and printing opportunities, and physical arrangements conducive to all stages of the writing process. *These essential tools should be provided in a way that levels the inequities that students bring from their lives outside of schools.*

With the role of writing instruction clarified within your larger responsibilities as a teacher and with these guiding principles for a writing workshop in mind, let's now turn to some of the decisions that you must make to give your writing workshop the structure necessary to be effective.

Teaching Writing— Daily Structures to Thrive and Survive

To address the daily teaching of writing—what it looks like in the real world—I have to stress once again that an authentic writing program that empowers students and grows from a workshop metaphor requires *structure* as modeled by Ray and Laminack (2001) and Atwell (1998), among others. Refuting the traditional approaches to writing instruction, which tend to be decontextualized and inauthentic, does not imply an embracing of classrooms characterized by anarchy and entirely naturalistic learning. Student-centered instruction and students performing from their own choices, practicing their own freedoms, are not in conflict with a well-organized and highly structured classroom; in fact, I argue that those qualities enhance one another.

Yet no hard and fast templates exist—just guiding principles. A series of questions will be explored here with some specific examples offered as possible answers, but I must caution that the questions are far more important than any prescriptive answers. These questions will offer a framework for designing your writing program or workshop regardless of the age of the students, the setting within which you teach, or the weight of writing instruction within your course requirements. Further, these questions address real-world, day-to-day issues that often can impede effective writing instruction if left unaddressed or handled randomly.

How should I assign compositions? How many compositions should be required per grading period? First, these key questions must be answered within the context of some of the guiding principles already discussed. If we are to honor student choice and empowerment, the term "assignment" takes on a slightly different meaning when compared to traditional approaches to assigning work. Assigning compositions, here, means that a degree of negotiation takes place between a teacher and her students within the larger goals of a course. In effective writing instruction, an "assignment" should avoid being coercive and being merely a template to be completed by a passive student. That said, within a writing workshop teachers still have writing assignments that tend to be characterized by student choice and by having students work fully throughout the stages of the writing process. Some options and considerations follow.

- Frame your writing assignments over a grading period so that students have at least one week to work on an original piece and at least an additional week to rewrite after receiving teacher feedback. The amount of time you choose may vary, but be sure to allow enough time for students to implement the writing process in an authentic way; telling students to "write an essay for tomorrow" simply fails to meet the basic conditions within which writers work. For example, within a fairly traditional setting of nine-week grading periods, I often required students to complete four major compositions spaced two weeks apart for the initial submission of each composition; all of those four works were rewritten at least once as a requirement and more often by student choice.

- The assigning of major compositions must be accompanied by a rewriting policy; in my opinion the most effective writing instruction *both* requires and allows students to rewrite major works. All original compositions should be submitted with an initial rough and first-final draft that students are *required* to rewrite (after either peer or teacher input) at least once and are *allowed* to rewrite within parameters agreed upon between the teacher and student and within the restrictions of any grading period.

  A point of emphasis here—teachers of writing must implement rewriting policies to be effective, but that policy must emphasize that students place primary concern on *revising the content and stylistic elements of their compositions.* Teachers and students are better served by referring to the addressing of surface features (grammar, mechanics, and usage) as *editing,* not revision or rewriting. Editing is important, but only as a last step before a work is completed for final submission to a teacher or for publication. If you award higher grades on compositions when students only address their surface features, you are giving them the false impression that those features matter more than the content, organization, and style of their writing. "I am not willing to teach the polishing and adornment of irresponsible, unimportant writing," LaBrant (1946, p.123) asserted, and her sentiment must guide the message writing teachers send students as they rewrite and revise their work.

- How you assign each composition may fall along

a spectrum that is driven by your expertise, the needs of the students, the requirements of the school or the state, or by a combination of these concerns. Students may be told that all compositions are driven by student choice in topic and form; they may be told that some are driven by choice while some have tethered choice (for example, a teacher may dictate a certain genre for a composition but allow the student choice in content or allow any genre for the composition but require that it deal with a specific piece of literature studied or a single topic for all students) or they may have a fairly structured and directed sequence to the assignments (for example, the first essay may be a personal reaction to a text, followed by a critical response to a persuasive text, followed by an original persuasive composition by the student; this sequence has a unifying purpose and organization that addresses a larger writing goal—understanding persuasive writing).

These suggestions are not exhaustive, but they do offer a solid foundation for assigning compositions; the teacher (and students) must know how many compositions will be completed within a grading period, how much time will be allowed for writing and rewriting, and what instructional goals or student needs the assignments fulfill. Before we move to the next question, let me offer a couple serious cautions about the ideas above and assigning compositions in general.

- Rewriting and revision are crucial to writing programs; students must learn to rewrite, revise, and edit their own work, and they must have opportunities to consider and implement the teacher's responses during their rewriting. If a teacher takes the time to respond to student writing, that student should have a chance to continue with a particular work. Two concerns come to mind here. First, very young children who are learning to handwrite are inhibited by their *physical* ability to write and rewrite. In writing activities for children in kindergarten through fourth grade, the teacher should be cautious to avoid forcing frequent (or any) rewriting since the act of handwriting can negatively impact the process. Second, for all students the rewriting requirement should not supercede a writer's right to abandon a work; let students quit a piece that is clearly failing to begin again.

- Balance and integrate the assigning of writing that is completely left to the student to create and that which is prompt driven. Authentic writing characterized by student choice in content and form must be the heart of a writing program, but students also need tethered-choice assignments and opportunities to wrestle with prompt-driven writing (since most standardized tests include the latter, I will discuss dealing with this in Chapter Four). Choice-driven writing allows the student to choose both content and form; assignments characterized by tethered choice may require a particular genre or instruct students to write each composition in a different genre each time, and they may offer some parameters for content as well—such as dealing with a particular topic or piece of literature. In contrast, the traditional prompt-driven assignment dictates both content and form, as in, "Write a letter to the principal arguing either for or against the school's new policy on study halls."

Ultimately, the assigning of writing greatly impacts both the effectiveness of writing instruction and the entire writing process. You must make your decisions about how to assign writing with your purposes in mind, taking into account the varying abilities and experiences of the students.

How should I mark and assess writing? Throughout my career as a writing teacher, I have been plagued about how best to mark student compositions and assign their writing grades, both throughout the writing process and as a final assessment. Essentially, I believe these two areas are a constant struggle; I'm not sure if an answer exists. But I will offer a few guidelines to help ease the struggle, guidelines that have grown from my own attempts, failures, and successes over twenty years of teaching writing. The following ideas are reflected in my own writing text for students, *Vivid Language* (Thomas, 2001b); as in my previous book I suggest that the concepts within the specifics are more important than the exact framework I have used:

- The physical marking of student work involves many concerns. Be sure that any time you mark student writing, students will be required and allowed to do something with those comments (Reeves, 2004). Intricate marking of a composition that is not going to be revised is a waste of time for both teacher and student. The physical aspects of marking student writing—where to mark on the draft, what color pen to use, when in the drafting process to mark, etc.—are important, but those decisions are relative to many things. The best advice I have is to experiment and to feel free to make changes as you see both positive and negative results from marking essays.

- You must devise a system for marking student compositions that is efficient for you, clear to the student, and part of a system that allows students to revise without the need for you to be physically present when the student rewrites. Over the course of several years, I created a system in which I place only numbers throughout a student composition; students can then refer to the corresponding section in my textbook which includes explanations and examples drawn from other students' compositions to guide their own revision. For example, I might place an "18" beside a paragraph in a student composition that is offering a critical analysis of a poem, but fails to provide any quotes from the poem. In my text, "18" designates that the paragraph lacks support or examples; alongside this explanation I provide sample paragraphs both lacking and including support or examples. Further, each number in my text offers revision strategies—add, delete, or edit; "18" suggests that students add in their revision.

My system may not be—and probably *is not*—the only system that works, but an effective writing teacher implements a marking system that has these elements: the physical marking of the composition is relatively quick for the teacher; the marking offers clear and specific responses to the writing for the students; and the students are empowered through the marking to complete many of their revisions, either alone or with peers, without the need for the teacher being present.

- The marking of student papers sends a clear message to students about *what matters;* therefore, teachers must be careful not to overemphasize surface features in their marking. Your marking system must address matters of content, organization, and style as the most important aspects of composition. One strategy to place the proper emphasis in your marking of papers is to mark only issues of content, organization, and style the first or first few times you respond to an essay, reserving the marking of surface features until you and the student agree it is time to submit the work for a final time. In other words, your initial responses to the student composition should *support and encourage* the need for the student to revise and rewrite, saving simple editing for a later step in the writing process.

- Along with marking, assigning grades to writing can be a struggle; actually, it is always a struggle. Some concerns include when to assign a grade to a piece and what to consider when assessing a student for a formal report card. I have used several strategies that shift with the makeup of the students and with my instructional goals. Some options I have chosen are as follows:

1. Only marking an initial final draft without assigning a grade; I withhold assigning a grade until a student revises this draft.
2. Delaying assigning a grade until a student declares a draft is her final submitted draft.
3. Grading each submission and choosing among the following options for assigning a composi-

tion its final grade: keeping the *last* draft grade only; averaging the last two grades as the grade for the piece; averaging all of the grades among the drafts as the final grade. Each of these options is appropriate according to the level of the students and the instruction goals for any grading period.

Of course, these grading options are greatly impacted by how your composition grades fit within your course and whether or not you implement portfolio or other authentic assessment strategies as part of your writing program.

As with marking, grading student writing also sends a clear message to students about what matters. I grade major works based on a three-tiered system and a twenty-point scale. The grading a student sees on her writing is based on this model:

C/O (content and organization)=10 pts.
D/S (diction and style)=5 pts.
G/M (grammar and mechanics)=5 pts.
20 pts.

This system places a great deal of emphasis (75% of the ultimate grade) on *what* the student expresses and *how* the student expresses it. The twenty-point scale I use correlates letter grades in three-point increments: 20–18 equals an A, 17–15 is a B, and so on. This grading has worked well for me, but I stress that whatever grading system you use, it is imperative that the grading reflects your instructional goals as a writing teacher. (How this grading structure is implemented and how it correlates with my marking of essays are fully detailed in *Vivid Language* [Thomas 2001b].)

How do I handle the paper load? Teaching writing effectively and authentically involves the marking and grading of student writing—and the weight of handling the paper load. NCTE has been active in addressing this concern, as well as the negative impact that facing a large paper load has on effective writing instruction. (A valuable resource on dealing with the paper load can be found through NCTE's web site along with position statements concerning the need for writing teachers to have appropriate student/teacher ratios that enable the teacher to perform the teaching of writing well.) Embedded in the discussion above is what I believe to be the most important element in dealing with grading large numbers of student compositions—creating and implementing an efficient marking system, such as the one I have described. Beyond your system for marking and grading compositions, a few other strategies can help offset the daunting task of handling the paper load.

- Plan writing assignment due dates and the submission of rewrites in a way that work comes to you at a reasonable pace (not all students have to turn in their compositions simultaneously) so you can return the work quickly. I always worked hard to return compositions the day after they were submitted, but that goal was possible only when I planned submission times well and correlated those submissions with instructional and assessment plans. If student writing trickled in, a few papers each day—instead of all one hundred papers at once—I was able to respond to and return them quickly.

- Plan instruction and classroom activities to allow for composition marking and grading *in class*—either in conferences with students or while students work independently or in groups without a need for direct teacher input. The workshop format can be structured to accommodate marking time for the teacher so that students receive nearly immediate feedback—which benefits both the teacher and the student.

- Balance the assigning of student work other than writing so that it does not overburden you with marking and grading the other work, thereby inhibiting your time and motivation to work with student writing.

- Assign writing and other student work that can simply be noted as completed; in other words, you don't have to read everything, and sometimes

work by a student simply receives a check. There is clear evidence that students benefit from the act of composing even when there is no direct input from their teacher. For a writing teacher to be effective, she must manage her time. None of us can do everything all the time. One of the great faults of teaching writing is attempting to do too much too often, which only creates a dynamic that insures disaster.

- Balance your composition marking and grading so that you do not mark and address everything in every essay. You might target one or two elements in a given composition, such as sentence variety or the use of figurative language. If your marking is targeted, you can simply ignore circumstances outside those targeted goals. (Note that it is imperative for you to inform students, parents, and administrators about targeted marking and assessing in writing, since an uniformed person might see an essay with many unmarked misspellings and a grade of "A," leading to misconceptions about the teacher and her expertise. Some teachers implement a stamp that states something such as, "This work is being assessed ONLY for _____ and _____.")

- Provide your students with one-draft writing exercises that are completed in class and that you mark holistically; you will not need to put comments throughout the work since they will not be rewriting. The grades should correspond to a detailed rubric so students can evaluate the specific strengths and weaknesses of their writing from the rubric (See Popham [2003] for invaluable help on designing rubrics).

- Set aside times when students assess each other's writing at some point within the drafting stages; well-designed rubrics—either by the teacher alone or with the students—will greatly improve the effectiveness of peer grading. Peer and group assessments of writing are extremely valuable activities for the students to develop their own sense of high-quality and effective writing—and these strategies save the teacher time.

- Designate a set of compositions periodically that requires students to self-evaluate their work; again rubrics should support this self-assessment.
- Negotiate opportunities to have other teachers grade a set of papers; a teacher in another content area or another school helps both you and your students gain insight into a different perspective on the students' work. Having someone else assess your student writing is also a valuable technique for monitoring the reliability of your own assessments of student performances.
- Have your students submit one set of compositions with an audiocassette tape which you can use to talk about each paper as you read it (In our digital age, other options may be available or your English department may want to invest in a set of small hand-held recorders). These oral responses are often quicker and a change of pace for both you and your students.
- Implement one-on-one or group conferences in place of marking a set of compositions. This can be done as part of class time or, when possible, as an out-of-class activity.
- When access is available for all students, use computers for storing student drafts and incorporate word-processing functions that allow editing and marking drafts by keyboard.
- A highly effective strategy that supports effective writing instruction and better overall instruction is to eliminate a great deal of the isolated vocabulary or grammar lessons and assessments that you implement as part of your ELA instruction. A great deal of time can be recaptured when you collapse the various reading and writing goals that are traditionally dealt with in isolated ways into holistic assignments and assessments.

Let's end this point with a couple of concepts that should guide us as we try to be wonderful writing teachers but also recognize our limitations of time and energy. First, to paraphrase and manipulate Thoreau, it is not our job as writing teachers to do everything, but to do *some*thing—and do that something as well as humanly possible. Often, as teachers, our drive to be perfect backfires and makes our work fail. So one guiding principle to handling the paper load is that we have to focus and accept that practices designed to manage the paper load are not cheating our students but in fact are helping them.

A second guiding concept is that it is far more important that students write than it is that we mark their papers. Hillocks (1995), in fact, discovered that free writing by students (writing daily and at length with no input from a teacher) correlated well with improvement in student compositions— significantly more so when compared to students who learned writing through direct grammar instruction.

What criteria guide writing assessment? Throughout this discussion, I have both stated directly and implied that writing teachers must be aware of what makes writing effective—and even brilliant. With that, I have argued that no templates exist to do so. Further, it is the job of a writing teacher to help young writers develop their own awareness of what makes writing excellent. In order for a writing teacher to both evaluate and ultimately teach student writers, *and* for young writers to become skilled writers, some characteristics must be acknowledged concerning what makes writing exceptional. Many gifted writers and teachers of writing have offered the qualities of great writing; for me, helpful works are by Williams (1990, 1997). The following qualities often characterize the best writing.

- *A command of the conventions of the language* characterizes the best works of writers. From surface features to the expectations of form and genre, skilled writers implement or reject conventions with *purpose*. As writing teachers, we must find balanced ways to help students gain awareness of these conventions so that they can write purposefully—in contrast with trying to write correctly. This characteristic is profoundly different than the traditional drive to make students memorize the rules of language. The best writers occasionally use the fragment in writing.

For effect. The purposeful manipulation of the sentence form—or any of the conventions of language use or forms—is an ability we want our students to develop.

- *A commitment to writing that is specific and vivid* characterizes the best work of writers. Writing within all genres is effective when it is specific, vivid, and clear. The best writers work with details, prefer the concrete to the abstract, search relentlessly for the best and most accurate word or phrase, and offer rich elaborations, examples, evidence, and references.

- *A complex awareness of prose (governed by sophisticated understandings of sentence and paragraph formations) and poetic (governed by sophisticated understandings of line and stanza formations) expression* characterizes the best work of writers. Broadly, all writing falls somewhere in the world of prose or poetry; sophisticated and purposeful manipulations of sentences and paragraphs or lines and stanzas are the essential tools of the writer. As with the conventions of the language, *purposefulness* is central to how skillful writers form their sentences and paragraphs, their lines and stanzas. That purposefulness at the skilled level is *not* driven by complying with the rules but by how effective the strategy is in expressing the content of the writing.

- *Expressing a coherent and significant focus* characterizes the best work of writers. All effective writing makes some point or series of points. Writing is a vehicle for expression from the writer to some audience; it is not a demonstration of compliance with conventions. Without meaning, no other aspect of writing matters.

- *Coherence of form and genre along with coherence and appropriateness of voice* characterizes the best work of writers. So much of what makes a great piece of writing work involves a combination of elements that cannot be prescribed but can be described in that combination. The many choices writers make concerning form, genre, and voice ultimately impact the effectiveness of the composition in terms of how appropriate those choices and combinations are to the intent of the writer. The role of the writing teacher is to help evolving writers gain an increasingly greater sensitivity to and awareness of the many nuances that impact choices of form, genre, and voice.

- *Originality and sincerity* characterize the best work of writers. Since the most important aspect of written expression is the content of the work, the writing teacher must continually emphasize that all writing should be original and sincere. Written expression is easily fabricated (even more so today with the access we have to the Internet and virtually an endless bank of writing from which to rob) and easily manipulated. Young writers must be encouraged to craft new pieces—and given ample instruction in the many different systems of documentation—and to write with the best of intents.

What procedures enhance an effective writing program? How should students submit their compositions? Since I have already stressed the need for a systematic approach to writing instruction, I will add here a clear need for procedures and assessment structures (such as portfolio assessment) to insure effective writing instruction. Again, I believe a great deal of flexibility exists in some of the decisions about procedures and assessment, but the decisions need to be made, and made clear to students, parents, and administrators. First, let's consider a few concerns about procedures:

- *How should writing assignments be formatted?* I believe the physical guidelines of a submitted piece of work are often stressed so often by writing teachers that students come to believe that the formatting of the document is more important than the content of the writing. Yet guidelines are needed; just be sure to keep a proper perspective on those guidelines—such as *never* including conforming to those guidelines in the grading of the writing. The most important aspect of how to format writing submission is allowing enough space on the document for reactions by teachers and peers; I ask that typed documents follow standard formatting—double-spaced, 12-point reasonable fonts, adequate margins of 1 to 1.5 inch—and that handwritten submissions be written on every other line (skipping a line to make room for comments).

- *How should writing assignments be submitted?* It may seem trivial at first, but how students turn in their writing can make or break a writing program. A few essentials guide how I ask for work to be submitted. First, I make sure I have a system for labeling each submission from 1 through 16 (for my classes, four essays each of the four quarters during an academic year)—with a simple E.1, E.2, etc., system established for "essay one," "essay two." I then make sure that rewrites are clearly labeled; for example, the first full submission of essay one is labeled E.1, with a full rough and final draft submitted. After marking or responding to that essay in some way, I have the student rewrite, labeling the first rewrite E.1RW. As the student continues to rewrite, she simply adds numbers to the newer drafts—E.1, E.1RW, E.1RW2, etc. I require meticulous labeling of each draft's date of submission to keep a record of when the works are completed, which is essential to keeping a record of the drafts and their order. All of this information can be invaluable when conferencing with students and parents, or determining final grades.

- *Now, how do students and the teacher handle all these drafts?* I require all drafts of each assignment to be submitted each time so I can look over the history of the composition. This is essential to my assessments and responses. But all those drafts can become incredibly cumbersome. The solution for me is to require that each major composition be submitted in 10" x 13" clasp envelopes; these envelopes generally can hold several drafts of an essay (including research papers and all the source material—which I will discuss later) and provide adequate room on the outside of the envelope for information on each draft.

Procedures such as the ones outlined above can offer a structure that will make dealing with the paper load bearable, but the writing teacher must also make some crucial decisions about how to negotiate the many grades from compositions that have multiple drafts.

How should I record and determine writing grades? Should portfolio assessment govern writing assessment? How are portfolios implemented? Many procedural decisions will mesh with ultimate decisions about recording and determining grades on each writing assignment and in the course. Regardless of how you determine essay or course grades, I believe you should record all drafts and their corresponding grades (or notations that the draft was completed, if not directly graded) for each assignment, including when those drafts are completed. This record can be invaluable when determining overall performances and degrees of growth by writing students. If writing assignments are a part of a larger course or if writing is the central objective of a course, you may wish to include a **portfolio assessment** of writing to give your writing instruction greater coherence than simply calculating each essay grade among all other work would provide. Determining grades and managing portfolio assessment will include the following concerns:

portfolio assessment

When students organize a series of assignments into a coherent portfolio that is submitted for assessment.

- If you choose a portfolio-assessment strategy, you need to clarify what type of portfolio assessment is best for your instructional goals and objectives. Broadly stated, portfolio assessment can fall along a spectrum from **showcase portfolios** to **process portfolios**. In the showcase portfolio, teachers and students design a framework within which students choose a specified number and type of original works to be submitted at the end of a grading period as a showcase for their writing ability. This option has many strengths, since it allows the assessment to focus on where students are at the end of an instructional period, and it empowers students to eval-

showcase portfolios

A type of portfolio assessment that asks students to select a few superior pieces from a body of work.

process portfolios

A type of portfolio assessment that asks students to compile all drafts of all writing assignments in order to represent the writing process as well as the final compositions.

uate and select among their own work. Process portfolios often include all of a student's written works, in all their drafts, in order to highlight the writing process for each work and all the works throughout the instructional period. A great deal of flexibility exists for teachers and students to decide what to include and how to display that work, but process portfolios emphasize the writing process, while showcase portfolios emphasize final products. The portfolio you choose, or any hybrid you design, simply needs to fit best what your goals are for that instructional period.

- For writing instruction—or any instruction that deals with student performances of holistic and authentic acts—I strongly recommend that you suspend your dependence on averaging assignment grades to reach final grades. As I noted above, showcase portfolios offer one key advantage—allowing an assessment to focus on where a student stands at the *end* of instruction. Averaging grades can greatly distort what a student has achieved by weighting early performances at a novice level equally to later performances at a more expert level of understanding.

No simple prescription exists for deciding how you manage and determine final grades on student compositions, but you must be certain that the assessment procedures respect the holistic and authentic act of writing, and that the assessment meets your instructional goals. Just as many traditional instructional strategies fail writing instruction, so do many traditional assessment procedures, such as averaging grades.

Direct Writing Instruction—A Time to Teach

David Peter Noskin (2000) explains that he struggled over the fifteen years it took him to move from what he learned about writing workshops in college to implementing authentic and student-centered writing instruction in his classrooms. But his journey shows that writing workshops embracing the concepts I have stressed here can be brought to life in *real* classrooms; it also shows that writing workshops do have direct, organized, and planned instruction: "[T]he answer was not to abandon the idealism. Instead, I began the process of adapting to meet the realities of high school," Noskin explains (p. 35). Now let's look at those realities of direct writing instruction in a writing workshop.

Four instructional concerns must be in place, or addressed in some way, as you plan and implement your direct instruction: distinguishing between *writing to learn* and *learning to write;* addressing *reading like a writer;* focusing on *craft lessons;* and determining the size of the instructional group (from individual conferencing to small-group conferencing to whole-group instruction). Let's look at each of these concerns before detailing many direct instructional practices that will be a part of your writing workshop:

- **Writing to learn *versus* learning to write**—while both of these strategies are important in a writing workshop, each has a different emphasis when it is the focus of your instruction. "Writing to learn" places an emphasis on writing as a learning tool; thus, be careful not to stress the writing itself when students are writing to learn. "Learning to write" is the dominant focus of virtually all of the direct-writing instructional strategies and areas I will detail later in this chapter. A "writing to learn" activity would be asking a student to respond to a primary document in social studies as a process for checking her understanding; a "learning to write" activity would be having a student write an original piece while implementing some of the strategies the writer of the primary document incorporated. Always be sure that students know which writing they are involved in—"writing to learn" or "learning to write."

- **Reading like a writer**—if any one guiding concept should anchor direct instruction in a writing workshop, it is this one. During my work with an affiliate of the National Writing Project, I

writing to learn

when a student uses the act of writing as a process for learning.

learning to write

Composing opportunities that allow students to practice writing, thus writing to learn to write.

reading like a writer

A holistic process that incorporates reading and writing. Using this strategy, students look at a rich piece of writing for both content (what it says) and craft (how the point is expressed). From the reading experience, students are encouraged to practice some of the crafts in their own original writing.

discovered over the course of three summers the power of fostering this skill in teachers who were attempting to be writers themselves for the first time. This is a strategy that works with the youngest student and the most experienced; kindergarteners can do this! Reading like a writer simply means looking closely at a text for both *what* is said and *how* the idea is expressed. Many of the instructional strategies that follow will address specific activities to foster reading like a writer in your students.

- *Craft lesson*—an extension of reading like a writer, at least in part, is helping students directly with implementing craft in their own writing. As students become more sophisticated about noticing literary techniques, rhetorical strategies, or conventions in the writing of others, they must be guided to apply those same strategies and experiments in their own work. "Craft," as a term, has traditionally been addressed in ELA through the discussion of literary techniques but includes any strategy a writer implements in writing for effect—including the manipulation of punctuation or sentence form.

- *From individual conferences to group instruction*— direct instruction can be implemented in a wide range or number of students addressed. Whether the direct instruction is aimed at a single student in a writing conference or is a whole-class lesson, the lessons and strategies that follow can be implemented with a great deal of success. That effectiveness, however, depends on the appropriateness of the instruction for the objectives and number of students, along with the sources for the direct instruction (based on student performances, drawn from demands of the state or of the field, or included as a part of the teacher's expertise in writing).

These concerns are helpful touchstones for guiding your decisions while you teach students to write; further, planning and implementing direct instructional strategies will also be shaped by the four concerns listed above.

Now I will discuss more closely a number of direct instructional ideas that will be central to the effectiveness of a writing workshop. I must add again that student-centered, authentic instruction allows and embraces direct instruction. Direct instruction is not in conflict with best practice (Zemelman, Daniels, & Hyde, 1998)—in other words, those practices supported by a body of research and by practitioners—but best-practice concepts *do* impact the role of direct instruction. It is not a matter of *if* something is directly taught, but *how* it is directly taught.

The decision to offer direct instruction will spring from three equally important and valid areas—student displays of interests and needs, the mandates of state or federal standards or assessments, and the expertise of the teacher based on the expectations of the writing field. Kohn (1996) speaks of "meaningful student choice within teacher-devised framework[s]"; that will be our framework for direct instruction (p. 111). The order of these instructional concerns are random, and they are probably not exhaustive, but I do feel that they are critical for an effective writing program. I have seen most of these concerns as both needs and interests of students; as primary issues of ELA departments, state departments of education, and federal mandates; and as integral concerns within the field of writing and for practicing writers.

Lesson 1—purpose and appropriateness. Two concepts that are universal in writing are purpose and appropriateness. They impact issues of content, organization, style, diction, and surface features. Once a writing teacher can move students away from black-and-white thinking, away from thinking about writing rules, she is well on her way to being an effective teacher.

Reading like a writer is a key strategy here. Students must begin to look closely at texts for what writers do (purpose) and how they do it (appropriateness). These elements combine to raise a guiding question for evaluating writing: "Do the writer's choices work in the context of their content and the impact of their writing on their audience?" These lessons can be along a wide spectrum—again from content and style issues to mere surface feature choices. A couple of examples can serve to illustrate the basic concept of lessons on purpose and appropriateness:

- One activity useful for students of any age is to take a text for analysis of purpose and appropriateness. This analysis could be modeled first by the teacher, who would select a brief passage with a clear tone and help students associate the purposeful selection of words (diction) that create the appropriate tone. A helpful extension of this close reading is to show how changing the word choice can alter the tone and create a conflict between meaning and tone. I once had a student who wrote a poem about the death of her cat; the student intended to be serious and hoped the poem would have a sad tone, but she had rhyme "cat" with "flat" when detailing that the cat had been hit by a car. The rhyme and use of the word "flat" were inappropriate for the purpose of the poem—to show sadness over the loss of a pet.

- I believe these concepts—purpose and appropriateness—are so crucial to teaching writing that I have them as central to my Golden Rule of Writing: "No rules exist in writing; only guidelines. But writers must have control of all that they choose to apply and must make each choice with a purpose that aids in the creation of meaning for the reader. Anything a writer applies for effect and with purpose is acceptable. Even fragments" (Thomas, 2001b, p. 7). Writing teachers must begin to teach the conventions of language—surface features—as relative choices made by writers with purpose. Not as fixed rules. Activities that allow students both to explain how and why writers use the surface features they do and activities that allow students to write while purposefully "breaking the rules" empower and help them gain an increasingly more sophisticated awareness of purpose and appropriateness.

diction

The choice of words by a writer.

*Lesson 2—**diction** (word choice).* Some direct lessons are big concepts; others deal with the smallest details. Few lessons are more important than making student writers meticulous about selecting the smallest elements of the writing craft—words. Direct lessons in diction overlap with other lessons—such as tone—but students benefit greatly from lessons that deal with words. In fact, if writing teachers would move away from isolated vocabulary instruction and toward diction instruction, students would be better served. The distinction between traditional, isolated vocabulary instruction and diction lessons as part of a writing program includes shifting to a focus on learning words to enhance the writer's purpose for a composition instead of learning a list of words prescribed by a teacher for the purpose of passing a test. Diction lessons can be both close readings and writing exercises that focus on word choice within the context of purpose.

Lesson 3—specificity and clarity. "Thoreau had strong feelings about slavery"—I don't care to recall how many sentences like this I have encountered over twenty years of teaching writing. But I know raising students' awareness that some key words and phrasings leave the reader wondering instead of enlightened is highly effective in writing instruction. "Feelings" is one such word, along with "how," "why," "idea," and dozens of other vague words we use when a more specific word would bring life and clarity to our writing. For writing instruction, the best strategy I have found is a relentless attacking of student habits that render their sentences vague, such as identifying words that leave the reader wondering instead of knowing. Thoreau didn't just have "strong feelings" about slavery; he rebuked slavery in all forms.

I would like to add here that I believe a longstanding approach to teaching writing has *mis*taught students habits that make their writing vague when we should be encouraging specificity and clarity. Traditionally, students are taught to follow an essay template—introduction with thesis, body, and conclusion. Within that framework they are often instructed to make *general* comments in the introduction, with support to follow in the body. A better approach is to offer students a guideline that is more authentic and that will produce much more vivid writing: Be specific from the beginning and elaborate! We'll deal with this more as we discuss writing forms.

Lesson 4—sentence/paragraph and line/stanza awareness. When I was in a prescriptive mode as a teacher, when I persisted in treating students as if they were empty vessels to be filled by my infinite wisdom, I often taught poetry by telling students upfront what the four or five characteristics of poetry are. This strategy often culminated in students writing terrible papers defining poetry. My imposed characteristics and their misunderstanding of them resulted in lifeless and inaccurate papers. Eventually, along with my students, I found that making an essential distinction about written expression was far more helpful for students as writers than any characteristics of poetry or prose. I began helping students to develop, over a long period of time, a greater and greater awareness about the distinction between poetry and prose—the central distinction between composing within the boundaries of sentences and paragraphs versus the boundaries of lines and stanzas. As a simple metaphor, I helped students see that all creative people work within artistic mediums—such as a visual artist choosing between drawing in pastels and working with clay. Prose expression is distinct from poetic expression—while both implement the same techniques (literary and rhetorical devices) and essential elements (words, phrases, and clauses), both defy any frozen definition. Poets tend to write with complete sentences (though students will claim differently), and some prose writers consider rhythm (John Gardner admitted to scanning his prose much as poets do!).

focus
The central point or points raised or addressed by a writer is the focus; traditionally, this concept is more commonly called a thesis.

coherence
Consistent and clear language, sentence and composition formation, and ideas.

*Lesson 5—**focus** and **coherence**.* Much as I claim that the teaching of the traditional essay form and guidelines such as "begin with general statements" are inauthentic and ultimately harmful to student writers, I also believe that our traditional concern for overtly stated thesis sentences does more harm than good. The truth is that effective writing has some focus and some degree of coherence, but that focus and coherence come from a variety of sources, only one of which is a directly stated thesis sentence. The single best focus and coherence lesson I have ever used involves a piece of writing that depends on irony; for years I used an editorial by Mike Royko dealing with the flag-burning issue. In the piece, he satirizes being in favor of a Constitutional amendment banning the burning of the flag. Satiric pieces show students that focus and coherence can be achieved in many effective ways that are indirect. In fact, the great majority of excellent pieces achieve both focus and coherence subtly—not blatantly. (The Royko piece, for example, rejected the idea of banning flag burning—though it never directly stated so and in fact appeared to state just the opposite to the careless reader who missed the tone.)

Lesson 6—support and evidence. One of the most common reactions I received from students when I stressed the importance of being specific from the beginning in their writing was that they found themselves saying what they meant in the first paragraph, thus having nothing else to say! This taught me that the template approach to essay writing, combined with teaching students to begin with general statements to be supported later, results in teaching students very bad habits as well as a number of misconceptions about writing. To give students something to write after they begin by being specific in their writing, a truism is that support and evidence are what make writing vivid; good writing is filled with detail-rich support and evidence, whether that writing is poetry or prose, fiction or informational. A wide variety of writing exercises enhance this lesson.

Students who wrestle with a variety of genres and forms that require support and evidence come to see that those components make all writing *concrete;* without support and evidence, most student writing remains abstract and lifeless. Direct lessons can show students that support and evidence come in a wide variety of forms—statistics, stories (fictional and true), quotes and references from other sources, hypothetical examples, and more. Of course, reading widely helps students build a toolbox of strategies for infusing their writing with support and evidence.

Lesson 7—elaboration and development. Support and evidence are slightly narrower elements of a larger weakness found in novice writing—a lack of elaboration and development. Once students have been sold on the value of support and evidence, they are apt to persist in offering a single example for any point. Elaboration and development as writers' tools are often best approached through fiction passages. Students are more comfortable with the need to tell a story with a degree of richness that they may see as unnecessary in their own informational or academic writings. Gardner (1991), though he is specifically discussing fiction, argues for the essential nature of writing—creating a "vivid and continuous" dream in the reader's mind (p. 31). In other words, all writers seek to engage the reader so that the reader suspends, at least momentarily, the abstract and arbitrary acts of writing and reading—mere black print on white paper. As humans, we know that *living* is far more engaging than *reading;* thus, writing which is most effective creates something like an experience through words. Elaboration and development are crucial to cast a writer's spell—to engage readers through the written word *as if* the reader has lived through what has been written.

Lesson 8—surface features (conventionality). Yes, we can and should do direct instruction of surface features. That comes with only a few caveats. Two types of direct grammar/mechanics/usage instruction are very effective *if* that instruction is intended to improve those areas of student writing—individual lessons based on evidence of student weaknesses in their own original writing and group lessons based on the same. For instance, if a student shows persistent problems with confusing pronoun cases, that student needs direct instruction, though being more concerned about a child's ability to identify the case of "whom" instead of being able to choose between "who" and "whom" when she needs to conform to conventionality probably doesn't serve that student well. To take another example, if a large group of students or a whole class shows a particular problem area—such as choosing "they" and "them" as the pronoun to refer to singular but non-specific nouns such as "student"—then a teacher should clearly address this as whole class instruction. *Direct instruction of surface features is highly effective in improving grammar, mechanics, and usage in student writing when the sources of the instruction are original student compositions.*

Additionally, surface-feature direct instruction can be culled from reading activities where students examine professional pieces closely to see how and why writers implement (or reject) conventional surface features. Some of my best lessons have been similar to this: Take an article from *Triathlete* magazine and write guidelines for comma usage based on how the commas are used in this article; include examples from the article for all your guidelines.

genre
The forms that compositions take fall into categories. Broadly, the genres are divided into prose and poetry or fiction and nonfiction. In more specialized references, the genres are fiction (both book-length and short fiction), poetry, nonfiction, and drama.

*Lesson 9—writing form and **genre**.* For many years, I taught tenth-grade ELA at a high school that was tenth through twelfth grades; so my tenth-graders came to me from junior high with a large bank of ideas about writing. One of my first activities each year with those students was to have them directly attack many of their assumptions concerning writing forms and genres; an early activity was to have students gather a number of publications—including books, magazines, and newspapers—and analyze the writing for traditional introductions or thesis sentences along with their own assumptions about required numbers of sentences per paragraph.

Writing instruction throughout modern American education has been dominated by what I often call a "template" approach to writing—analogous to teaching art by having students paint by numbers.

This approach is grounded in the assumption that novices need a tight structure to begin with, and that with time those students can be given more freedom. Two problems exist with this assumption: first, there is no compelling evidence that all beginners need imposed and simplified templates to learn authentic performances; second, once a tight formula has been ingrained in young writers, few ever take the opportunity to experiment or move beyond the formula.

In place of template approaches to writing forms and genres, students need a large variety of opportunities both to read many different writing forms and genres and to experiment with those forms in their own writing. Instead of mandating an introduction (with a bluntly stated thesis), body, and conclusion, teachers should help students explore the many varied approaches writers use to organize and develop a piece of writing. Yes, all writing begins some way, continues some way, and ends some way (although sometimes those beginnings or endings are implied), but the traditional school essay form—whatever hybrid of the five-paragraph essay is in vogue—is an inauthentic and rare thing (I would argue that if it weren't imposed falsely in classrooms, it wouldn't exist at all!). In place of teaching the essay template, you need to design dozens and dozens of activities where students explore and experiment with beginnings, middles, and ends as they are most effective throughout a wide variety of genres. Narrative fiction beginnings can be quite different from one piece to the next, quite distinct from the opening stanza of a poem, and quite unusual when compared to a newspaper editorial. Yet, if we look closely, fiction writers, poets, and journalists all do many things exactly the same.

As has been stated in other sections, students who are learning to write—even in matters of form and genre—need to develop a sense of appropriateness. A persuasive piece might begin with a narrative episode and hold any stated thesis until the end quite effectively. It is not the role of the writing teacher to impose writing forms; it is our job to assist young writers as they discover and develop the many varied concepts that guide writing forms, genres, and the effectiveness of written expression. When students are bombarded with writing instruction that is rule intense and template driven, they develop disproportional concerns for those rules and lose sight of what makes writing wonderful.

Initially, my students often asked about writing on the back of paper, writing past the pink-line margin, how many sentences I required in paragraphs, and other such non-issues. These misplaced concerns were the results of template-based writing instruction. When students begin coming to you with two different beginnings to a personal narrative and asking which one best establishes the tone of the piece, then you have begun teaching students about writing forms and genres. Students do need direct instruction in writing forms, but those lessons need to be discovery and experimental lessons about authentic forms, not lessons that impose false templates—especially false templates to appease standardized testing (which we will discuss in the next chapter).

Lesson 10—writing process. To be honest with students, writing teachers must admit that writing forms are varied—too numerous to enumerate or to prescribe for students. We must also admit that there is *a* writing process, not *the* writing process. It is common to reduce instruction to linear and sequential processes because ordered steps are easier to manage. But producing a piece of writing cannot and should not be reduced to a lock-step process since that is not how real writers work.

What, then, should our direct instruction of the writing process deal with? An essential paradigm shift must occur concerning how we approach the writing process: We must move *away* from imposing linear, uniform, and prescribed steps on students ("Today we will all brainstorm the introduction to our personal narrative by webbing . . .") and *toward* allowing each student a number of opportunities to discover her own writing process, noting that each writer may have a different writing process. Direct instruction in the writing process should include exposing students to a large bank of prewriting, drafting, revising, and editing strategies from which they choose through experimentation and conferencing with their peers and the teacher. All writers somehow generate ideas and make decisions; all writers somehow produce drafts, and all writers somehow produce final forms, but the *how*'s vary widely and are dependent on how successful that writer's final piece is. As a professional writer for twenty years, I have never done a web to brainstorm; I have never produced a formal outline, and I enjoy brainstorming, revising, and drafting simultaneously *while* I draft at the keyboard.

John Irving claims he writes the ends of his novels first; John Gardner believed in creating characters and following them through the drafting. The writing process any writer follows is an idiosyncratic thing that cannot and should not be prescribed; there is no one best way, except the way each student discovers and refines for herself as she grows as a writer. Direct instruction dealing with the writing process should be an opportunity for teachers to expose students to a wide variety of options for moving from generating ideas to completing a piece of writing. But how each student will proceed cannot be predicted and must not be prescribed.

Lesson 11—research/inquiry writing and documentation. While too often we focus writing instruction on forms that are unique to academia, writing teachers should be concerned with some of the expectations of the academic world—notably documentation and source-rich writing. I exited my K–12 and undergraduate schooling well versed in proper MLA documentation, but my real lessons in source-based writing and documentation came when I began writing at the graduate level and for publication, which led to my discovering a puzzling array of documentation formats. The goal of the traditional research paper project in schools should shift from making the format of MLA (or any other system) and following a process the goals of instruction. Instead, we need to foster an understanding in students of scholarly writing that involves sources, of the concept of documenting the use of other people's words and ideas, and of the implementation of documentation formats, regardless of which format is used. Just as I have had students more concerned with writing on the back of paper than with what they expressed *on* paper, I have students far more concerned about following a traditional outline ("If you have an 'A,' you must have a 'B' . . .) and formatting the proper-sized note card correctly than avoiding a cut-and-paste (and thus pointless) research paper.

Lesson 12—agreement and parallel forms. An ideal approach to direct instruction that avoids the inherent problems with imposing through teaching is to seek broad concepts that are as generalizable as possible. Too often, we teach the conventions of English grammar, mechanics, and usage as black-and-white rules—when, in fact, they are quite pliable. One truism is that the English language thrives on agreement and parallel forms—subject-verb agreement, pronoun-antecedent agreement, and parallelism, for example. When students begin to see the patterns of agreement and parallel forms, they begin to gain power over the language instead of it controlling them. Look for assignments that have students explore the many forms of agreement and parallelism found in engaging pieces of writing; taking a cue from James Kilpatrick and other conservative grammarians, have students scan newspapers and magazines for examples of writers carelessly breaking the conventions of agreement and parallelism. While many English conventions defy logic—the use of "aren't I," for example—agreement and parallelism are highly logical and consistent throughout the language; these activities can be used to give students the sort of stability they enjoy and need to grow as writers.

*Lesson 13—**style**, **voice**, and **tone**.* Simply put, for students developing style, voice, and tone is far

style

The cumulative quality of the writer. Often, the components of a writer's work that most directly affect style are diction, subject preferences, tone, voice, sentence formation, genre, and craft.

voice

The quality of the narrator, speaker, or author who is either literally or figuratively speaking through the words.

tone

The attitude of the narrator, speaker, or author toward the subject of the writing.

more important than knowing where commas go. Of course, having a command of the conventions is a *part* of style, voice, and tone, but we must make sure that we seek writing activities that foster in students a sensitivity to style, voice, and tone in the works of great writers as well as in their own experimentations with developing style, voice, and tone as growing writers. These are the most integrated activities you will implement—mining the work of great writers for examples to emulate in original pieces.

These lessons are *big concepts* that embrace a number of smaller writing concepts such as diction, figurative language, syntax, and virtually every trick available to a writer. Thus the importance of these direct lessons! Choose activities that focus around having students identify style, voice, and tone in short passages; then ask students to explain *how* the writer achieves each. The *how* is as important as identifying the style, the voice, or the tone. Further, students should be asked to write using those same techniques to develop their own array of styles, voices, and tones. Creative-writing activities such as those suggested by Gardner (1991) are excellent sources of writing exercises—ones that can be adapted to other genres as well.

Lesson 14—conciseness. Joseph Williams (1990) offers a wonderful example of teaching writing by broad concepts—one of which is the central nature of conciseness in writing. As a young writer-in-progress during my undergraduate days, I learned to write because of the relentless pursuit of conciseness by Dr. Predmore, one of my English professors who made the greatest impact on me as an evolving writer. This was his mania, and from it, I developed more than a sense of wordiness and emptiness; I learned to look closely at what I wrote and recognized that a significant relationship exists between what you write and how you phrase it—a brilliant or poignant idea poorly stated becomes a poor idea. As a writing teacher, I found myself passing on to my students that same attention to detail, firmly grounded in the concept of conciseness. Why write "all of a sudden," when "suddenly" can do the job in one word? Why write "stand up" or "sign up," when "stand" and "register" do the jobs so much more eloquently? Part of me has come to realize that when we make our students aware of the effectiveness of concise writing, we are moving them toward the beauty and economy of expression found in the highest form of writing, poetry. All writers benefit from working to make every single word count. Additionally, lessons in conciseness are reinforcing the concept of purposefulness as well.

Lesson 15—organization. That organizational decisions impact the content of writing is a central concept to becoming a strong writer. Students need direct instruction on the many organizational options writers have, on the importance of matching one's organization with one's message in effective ways. Direct instruction in organization is *not* telling students to implement this or that organizational strategy—such as the handy five-paragraph essay template. Students need to read and analyze closely many different organizational patterns in a range of genres; poets and journalists often share similar organizational strategies, and students need to discover this. An effective strategy for reinforcing a student's perception of organization is a writing exercise that asks students to write the same piece three or four different ways, changing only organizational strategies.

Lesson 16—show, don't tell. Little has become more overstated, but little is truer than telling developing writers to show, but not to tell. However, this truism is often limited to poetry and fiction. In fact, it is a vital concept to all writing. "Show, don't tell" embraces a key tool of the writer—to make mere words come to life, to take the flat world of black-and-white print and give it the vibrancy of three dimensions and *living*. Simply put, the multi-textured image will always stay with a reader longer and more deeply than a flat statement. Again, the best strategy for fostering the ability to show in young writers is having them search the work of great writers for examples. An interesting inverted activity is to take a highly effective passage that shows and have students reduce it to what it is telling—deflating the balloon, as it were.

Lesson 17—speaker/narrator. All writing is the expression of *someone;* thus, all writing has a speaker or narrator (who may be in some works the author), whether subtle or overt and intrusive. Tone, point of view, and a whole host of key elements in a piece of writing are driven by choosing who the voice behind the writing is and by maintaining control of that voice. Writers need to both discover their own voice and develop the ability to create an array of speakers or narrators as is needed for different pieces, different messages, or different genres. Again, instructional attention to speakers and narrators is often limited to poetry and fiction, but young writers always need to be aware of who is behind any piece of writing—even a critical essay on *The Scarlet Letter.* All writing and all readers deserve a writer who pays close attention to the person behind the writing, the personality of the speaker or narrator.

This discussion of direct writing instruction is a foundation for the big ideas that most writers either need as introductions or as reinforcements or elaborations. One purpose of this discussion has been to stress the need for direct instruction as an integral part of a workshop where student choice and flexibility are valued.

Reconsidering the Discussion So Far

Once again, let's turn a critical spotlight on the discussion in this chapter. What does writing instruction look like in a real classroom? The truth is that effective writing instruction is highly structured, and even some of the instruction is teacher centered and narrowly directed. Does that reality refute the stated allegiance to constructivist and democratic principles offered so far? I think not. Structure and organization do not inhibit constructivist and democratic principles in the classroom; the structure

actually allows those goals to be achieved.

But I do believe that the reality of teaching writing is highly complex. The drive to simplify has hampered teaching in general and the teaching of writing specifically. If you teach writing well—even if you make all the right decisions and create all the right structures to support that instruction—it will still be sloppy, noisy, and fraught with fits and starts.

Now, with some idea of what writing instruction looks like in the real world, let's turn our attention to the expectations and impositions on that real world from standards and high-stakes testing of student writing.

Glossary

coherence—Writing achieves coherence by being consistent and clear in language, sentence and composition formation, and ideas.

craft lessons—Lessons that deal with a writer's use of purposeful techniques. A writer's craft includes literary technique, diction, syntax, and style along with virtually any strategy that writers use to manipulate and control meaning.

diction—The choice of words by a writer.

focus—The central point or points raised or addressed by a writer is the focus; traditionally, this concept is more commonly called a thesis.

genre—The forms that compositions take fall into categories. Broadly, the genres are divided into prose and poetry or fiction and nonfiction. In more specialized references, the genres are fiction (both book-length and short fiction), poetry, nonfiction, and drama. The term is often used in many flexible ways, but always refers to the broad qualities that separate written expression.

learning to write—Composing opportunities that allow students to practice writing, thus writing to learn to write. This process is in contrast to writing to learn, when writing is a learning strategy.

mini-lessons—Lessons of about ten to fifteen minutes that are planned and directed by the teacher. This concept is often associated with Atwell (1998); the teacher uses a brief lesson as punctuated directed lessons within the context of a workshop where students are highly active. For example, a teacher might plan a few mini-lessons throughout the year during reading workshops to introduce students to a series of authors. The mini-lesson is often teacher-centered, and may include traditional lectures.

portfolio assessment—When students organize a series of assignments into a coherent portfolio that is submitted for assessment, they are assembling portfolio assessments. Often, portfolio assessment can come in many forms, such as process or showcase portfolios.

process portfolios—A type of portfolio assessment that asks students to compile all drafts of all writing assignments in order to represent the writing process as well as the final compositions.

reading like a writer—A holistic process that incorporates reading and writing. Using this strategy, students look at a rich piece of writing for both content (what it says) and craft (how the point is expressed). From the reading experience, students are encouraged to practice some of the crafts in their own original writings.

showcase portfolios—A type of portfolio assessment that asks students to select a few superior pieces from a body of work.

style—A cumulative quality of the writer. Often, the components of a writer's work that most directly affect style are diction, subject preferences, tone, voice, sentence formation, genre, and craft.

tone—The attitude of the narrator, speaker, or author toward the subject of the writing is the tone.

voice—The quality of the narrator, speaker, or author who is either literally or figuratively speaking through the words.

writing exercises—Brief assigned writing by students that have an instructional purpose other than a finished writing piece. They often have highly directed guidelines or prompts, and they may spring from teacher expertise, curriculum guidelines, or student needs.

writing to learn—When a student uses the act of writing as a process for learning. This process contrasts with opportunities for students to compose as acts of learning to write.

CHAPTER FOUR

High-Stakes Testing, Accountability, and Teaching Writing

"Number one: writing never gets easier, it gets harder. You can't repeat yourself," explained Tim O'Brien (1999) while giving the President's Lecture at Brown University. His comments as a professional writer support my own argument here that writing defies templates and formulas, that the *teaching* of writing must resist the urge to reduce writing to templates and formulas, and that the assessing of writing must not value programmed writing over authentic writing even when time and cost are involved. Over the past few decades the growth of the standards movement, combined with the increase in the frequency and weight of high-stakes testing, has begun to impact profoundly and negatively the instruction and assessment of writing. This chapter will address the dangers of the standards and high-stakes testing movement in relationship to writing instruction, and we will also discuss how teachers can and should implement best practice in writing instruction while also acknowledging the state and federal mandates that directly impact student success and teachers' professional responsibilities and security.

The Realities of Standards, High-Stakes Testing, and Student Writing

Dell'Angela (2004) reports on a teacher who fears one of her best student writers will fail the state standardized writing exam: "The person who grades that test will be a $10-an-hour temporary worker in a conference room in Tampa who spends about three minutes on each essay," she worries. And this is only one of the many troubling but real facets of the state of standardized testing and its impact on students learning to write.

The very nature of **standards** creates a standard form, even in areas that should not be standard. Additionally, the standards movement carries with it the weight of standardized assessment. The costs of implementing those standards and the subsequent testing are often high, so officials tend to migrate toward solutions which are less expensive instead of those that are most educationally sound. Computers, too, are increasingly becoming a major factor in the assessment of not only multiple-choice testing but also student compositions.

standards

In education, standards refer to the curriculum that has been identified by some agency as the official curriculum of a grade, a course, or a content area. Those standards are often linked to official assessments to identify student achievement in relationship to those standards.

The reality of the standards movement and increased testing includes the effectiveness of state assessment instruments as well as the growing dependence on computers and tests that are both more easily and quickly scored and cheaper to implement. At the state levels, the issues stemming from the accountability movement, as they impact writing instruction, include the following.

- Large-scale tests that are high stakes are incapable of "evaluat[ing] the infinitely variable craft of writing in an objective and mechanical way" (Dell'Angela, 2004). Possibly the greatest problem with state assessments of composition is that there is a profound gap between authentic writing (and the authentic assessment of writing) and traditional large-scale testing. Writing as a type of performance may simply be outside the effective range of standardized assessment in the same way that art or athletic performances are. I often joke—not so humorously—that we would all balk if high school football matches required teams to determine games by the ubiquitous bubble test!

- Since standardized testing is best at dealing with those things we have traditionally called "objective," the current focus on standards and high-stakes tests has created a renewed call for focusing on the surface features of student writing. Garner (2004) reports on such a debate in Texas and shows that changes in the SAT will also contribute to this trend. Writing instruction has suffered from the surface-feature debate for decades and has just recently started to shift the emphasis of writing instruction to holistic concerns (appropriately). The impact of standardized testing will quickly and greatly erode the progress that has been made, since assessing surface features is easier and less expensive than assessing composition. In conjunction with the point above, the elements of writing that do lend themselves to standardized testing might gain the greatest weight in that assessment by default, thus disproportionately emphasizing those features that mean the least in student composing. *We simply must not allow assessment to dictate what matters in student composing.*

- Texas also represents another growing problem with state testing in general and with its impact on writing in particular: states have become so concerned with basic skills and with making sure students do well on their test, that the overall quality of instruction is eroding, particularly for students who attend college. The irony is that teaching students to do well on state writing tests is increasingly producing less-competent student writers who are blindsided once they enter college (Markley, 2004; Adler, 2004).

Further concerns about testing and its impact on writing come from two powerful sources—the SAT and computer-aided test scoring. The 2005 revision of the SAT (Cloud, 2003) directly impacts writing instruction and bolsters the move to score student writing with computers. At the state level, computers are already gaining increasingly more power in the testing movement since computer-aided scoring is less expensive and more efficient than human grading (Riley, 2004; Hurwitz, 2004). The SAT revision impacts writing instruction both by including actual student compositions on the test (the brevity of the time allowed and the types of prompts used will certainly become the focus of classroom writing) and by returning the isolated grammar portion to the test in multiple-choice format. These revisions and the use of computers for scoring on national and state assessments will only increase the urge to teach templates for writing and to return to teaching surface features in isolation—both of which result in ineffective writing instruction and take valuable time from authentic writing instruction.

The future of writing instruction looks bleak under the weight of accountability. Sartwell (2004) represents a growing number of those concerned about authentic writing instruction who believe we are heading down the wrong path with national and state high-stakes assessments of writing. "The teaching of writing as a machine procedure gains momentum by the day," Sartwell warns. The result? "The people who create and enforce the templates are . . . people without understanding or imagination, lobotomized weasels for whom any effort of thought exceeds their strength," Sartwell concludes. And that leads to students who merely write by hand or type what someone tells them to express— and how to express it. Let's now look at that wrong-minded template approach and how it has gained a damaging foothold in the psyche of Americans and what they expect from writing and other literacy instruction.

Misconceptions about Instruction— "Can" Does Not Equal "Should"

A troubling chicken-and-egg question faces us as we try to decipher the source of approaches to standardized assessments of writing. Have our assumptions about writing and the testing of writing impacted the practices of state and national testing, or have the tests forced us to see writing and writing assessment as we do? A larger and more pressing issue is that now, through No Child Left Behind legislation, many of these assumptions have become law and carry the weight of federal punishments.

Typical of the assumptions driving writing instruction is a report from Walzer (2004) concerning the template-driven writing instruction at Maury High School in Virginia. A common perception about the teaching of writing is that young writers must be forced to produce highly structured and directed writing before they are allowed to write by choice in form and content. As I have discussed throughout this primer, that assumption is false. *That students* can *be trained to write canned essays does not mean that we should do such—even when such a practice seems to support the federal and state standards we must address and even when it fulfills the requirements of high-stakes tests.*

"Can" does not equal "should," in other words. Regardless of the source, the common perceptions of writing instruction have now been codified through federal legislation and institutionalized through high-stakes tests. While many leaders in literacy are beginning to refute federal mandates about reading and literacy instruction and assessment (Krashen, 2004; Allington, 2004), we must include the dangers that NCLB and testing pose to writing specifically, since the focus on writing is gaining momentum, and writing instruction is heading for the same problems that have been faced by reading for decades. *Once writing becomes solidified as an integral part of high-stakes testing—alongside reading and math—the potential for problems increases dramatically.*

The teaching of reading has been plagued by ideological wars that do little to help any single child read. That dynamic has been fueled by assessment as well. Writing can expect the same pointless wars to increase as writing becomes more and more a part of the chosen curriculum—typically identified by its being heavily and often assessed in standardized ways.

We certainly *can* force students to paint by numbers in their art classes and produce increasingly better faux Picassos, but *should* we if our goal is to foster young artists? No. And as long as painting is not included on the SAT or state assessments, I believe there is little chance that template approaches to art will begin to grow in our schools. But it *is* happening with writing instruction, and the evidence is beginning to mount that it is destroying that instruction.

Standardized Tests of Writing—What Students Are Asked to Do

One problem with standardized tests of writing tied to accountability measures is the assumption that tests expect this or that—without verifying those assumptions. I have found that many fears about tests that drive instruction are baseless. I have noted the dangers posed to effective writing instruction by high-stakes tests, but I also need to reiterate that the reality of high-stakes testing of writing will not soon disappear, so the real expectations of students as writers must be addressed. What, then, do the typical standardized tests of writing ask students to do? Some common characteristics of high-stakes assessments of writing are as follows:

■ *Standardized tests of writing occasionally assess through selected-response formats and focus on editing skills dealing with surface features.* For many years, multiple-choice grammar and usage tests stood as the only form of so-called writing assessment. Gradually throughout the 1980s and 1990s, more high-stakes tests asked students to compose original samples, but many still included selected-response sections. Recently, the high cost of scoring written samples has accelerated a move back to selected-response tests being considered assessments of writing. In 2005, this trend will get a boost with the return of a multiple-choice test of surface features being added to the SAT. This reality will require that we find ways to help students increase their ability to edit the writing of others. The challenge is to find authentic ways to address an inauthentic assessment within a writing program. If students are assessed in this way, then we have to address the situation. What we must do is not let the poor tests negatively impact our bigger purposes as writing teachers.

- *Standardized tests of writing often reward template writing.* As the work of Hillocks (2003) and others has shown, most state assessments of student writing samples are driven by sample essays and rubrics that reinforce basic templates of essay form. Again, I warn that these templates should not become the writing program, but I add that students should be made aware of the template rewarded by the test as one form of situational writing, needed only on the test.

- *Standardized tests of writing often are prompt driven.* The best writing programs value student choice, but most standardized tests give students both the content and the genre through a prompt. When students are required to take such tests, they need practice in this sort of writing—but, not as the whole writing program.

- *Standardized tests of writing often have time limits.* With the new writing sample on the 2005 SAT, time limits will be brought into focus. The SAT will ask students to write one-draft essays in twenty minutes; the Advanced Placement English tests ask students to complete 3 essays in a total of 120 minutes. Students need time-restricted writing activities; often these time-limited writing samples also require students to write only one draft. Usually, authentic writing has almost no time limits and requires many drafts, but standardized tests ignore what is authentic. A responsible writing program gives students experiences with timed, one-draft writing.

- *Standardized tests of writing are often highly genre specific.* Most state standards for writing break the form into four or more genres and then ask students to demonstrate awareness of one of those through a writing sample. However the state assessment sees the genres, students must be aware of those distinctions. In many tests, a premium is placed on persuasive writing.

- *Standardized tests of writing are sometimes linked to reading passages.* The prominent NAEP test of writing requires students to read before writing; the significance of this practice is that such practices make assessing writing ability *alone* impossible since the sample may be negatively impacted by the students' reading ability.
- *Standardized tests of writing occasionally punish template writing.* The rubrics and scoring guidelines for the Advanced Placement English tests actually suggest that template writing, particularly the five-paragraph essay, is to be scored lower than writing that is non-traditional in its format. These rare but superior types of tests require that teachers know for sure the assumptions of the assessment.

The range of formats and assumptions that drive the standardized tests demands that teachers know the tests. The next step is to include in the writing instruction what students need without negatively impacting the whole writing program. The major point is that we must address fairly the realities of standardized tests, but we must do so with clarity since our students will encounter a broad range of expectations and assumptions as I have outlined above.

The Writing on the Wall—Research's Warnings

While there is a subtle irony here, the negative impact federal mandates are having on literacy education grows from a stated allegiance to research-based practices. However, research increasingly supports practices that *refute* the template approaches to teaching and assessing writing; this research suggests that the standards movement and high-stakes testing are negatively impacting writing instruction (Mabry, 1999; Freedman, 1991, 1995; Hillocks, 2003). These are the lessons we are beginning to learn from the negative impact of standards and high-stakes testing.

- The use and impact of rubric-driven writing instruction and assessment are negatively influencing authentic writing instruction (Mabry, 1999). Rubrics of a prescriptive kind directly support template-driven writing; the result is the canned writing we want to avoid. The use of rubrics to guide student writing or to identify assessment guidelines can have profoundly negative impacts on that writing. This research suggests that we need to look critically and closely at the use and formation of rubrics. Popham (2003) offers teachers ways to create rubrics that support learning instead of reducing student work to jumping through hoops.

- Sample essays provided by assessment companies and state departments quickly become the rubrics and templates teachers use for writing instruction. Soon, those samples *become* the writing program. A difficult paradox exists here. We know the power of examples in teaching and learning. In fact, I have suggested throughout this primer that we primarily expose students to a wide variety of beautiful writing as models. The evidence from research helps us, as with rubrics, to implement the use of sample essays carefully. Neither rubrics nor sample essays need to be excised from our classrooms, but we must make sure neither becomes a template for student writing.

- Writing for the test also soon becomes the entire writing program; instead of including the kinds of instruction and experiences students need to do well on state and national assessments as *part* of an overall authentic writing program, teachers are often teaching *only* template writing that fulfills the mandates of the tests students will encounter. This fact of schooling often trickles down as an administrative mandate—one that springs from good intentions. As writing teachers we must educate those who force the majority of class time to be spent dealing with the test that writing for a formal assessment is merely one small aspect of writing, one that can be dealt with within a larger and more effective writing program.

Hillocks (2003) has led a charge against the problems we are beginning to face, and he warns, "As a society, we cannot afford to spend valuable classroom time on vacuous thinking and writing. We need to tell citizens and legislators what these problems are and insist that they be addressed" (p. 70). In short, raising the standards of writing and increasing the assessment stakes for writing are further eroding writing instruction in America. While we must make this clear and work to change the conditions that are corrupting the authentic teaching of writing, we also must look at how writing teachers can teach writing well in the worst possible conditions.

Best Practice in Worst Cases—Avoiding the Traps

From Zemelman, Daniels, and Hyde (1998) to Weiss and Pasley (2004), we can state emphatically that we know what best practices are concerning the teaching of literacy skills; unfortunately, the mounting evidence suggests that federal and state mandates combined with popular expectations of schools create the worst possible atmosphere for implementing best practice. Further, that atmosphere also sets up students to fail in a number of real and disturbing ways. I want to turn now to looking at some of the broad characteristics of high-quality instruction (Weiss & Pasley, 2004) and discussing the good-student trap (Scheele, 2004); I will then offer some strategies for overcoming this intellectually paralyzing atmosphere through effective writing instruction.

Let's keep in mind the best practice strategies explored in Chapter Three and now place them in the broader context of high-quality instruction as described by Weiss and Pasley (2004). Despite two decades of raising standards and increasing accountability through more and more testing, American schools are, according to Weiss and Pasley's research on math and science, weak; research on states that are both standards and test intensive shows the same results, notably in Texas. If we wish to have effective classrooms, we must acknowledge that the political solution has not worked and will not work. Instead, we need classrooms with the following characteristics—which should form the foundation for best practice in writing instruction and should be bolstered by the writing program.

- *Excellent classrooms have high student engagement in their learning.* Accurate, rich content and direct instruction are pointless if students are not engaged with their learning. Again, writing instruction must primarily focus on student choice for their content and their genre; with choice comes higher engagement; with higher engagement comes deeper learning. As I have noted earlier, we need classrooms where students want to learn and perform for the sake of learning and performing. Classes with high expectations for authentic performances are classes with high intrinsic motivation.

- *Classroom environments must support a climate of learning.* When students and teachers are doing real things with real purpose—typically, a workshop focus—learning is enhanced dramatically. Many classroom management, instructional, and assessment strategies defeat their own purposes by being counter-educational. As we develop and implement writing instruction, we must be always careful *not* to squelch the central drive to learn that students must have supported by their teacher, their peers, and their school. Consider that the momentum of traditional schooling includes each class period beginning with a teacher having to ask the students to sit still and be quiet. What if students arrived in class each day to willingly begin their work without coercion? Self-directed students would do this and often do in the right circumstances. Engagement and empowerment are key here, but they must be fostered and valued by the teacher and even the entire school.

- *Effective classrooms provide all students equal access to learning.* The promises of democracy and a free society have always centered on the absence of discrimination. For public schools to begin fulfilling the promise of our democracy, we must be certain that our writing programs provide equal access to learning for all. The data on high-stakes testing and the mandates of NCLB both raise a red flag concerning that equal access. For writing instruction and high-stakes testing on writing, we must be certain that our instruction and testing do not merely become a way to sort students by their socioeconomic levels. A potential source of such a problem is the increasing use of technology—primarily computers—in writing instruction and assessment. We must be vigilant not to allow the increase in technology to provide an unfair and additional advantage for more affluent students in literacy instruction. There exists a long history of sorting students early in their schooling, often by their relative verbal abilities which are greatly impacted by their socioeconomic status.

- *Effective instruction is characterized by effective questioning.* Weiss and Pasley (2004) describe "effective questioning [as] that kind that monitors students' understanding of new ideas and encourages students to think more deeply" (p. 26); questioning that requires simple recall or yes/no answers is not effective. The role of teacher responses to student writing is essential here. We can both implement effective questions to improve our writing instruction and use effective questioning to make our students better students overall. In writing instruction, questions need to be open ended, and they need to encourage students to elaborate—focusing on the *why,* not the *what.* For example, we might begin asking students why they did something in an essay, being careful to ask that question both when they have made errors and when they have done something brilliant. Too often students elaborthat all teachers'questions signal errors. Questioning should become a way to allow students to elaborate and make their ideas public—not simply a way to once again tell them they have made a mistake.

- *Effective classrooms have direct instruction.* As mentioned before, student-centered classrooms still require expert teachers who often directly instruct. I will explore this further in Chapter Five, but the most effective writing teachers live some sort of writing lives themselves. From that experience, writing teachers have more effective instructors when they need to teach directly. Direct instruction is not a flawed instructional strategy, but the source of such teaching is often a problem. The direct instruction of isolated grammar fails because it doesn't spring from anything authentic in the students' writing. Direct instruction of grammar issues that *have* occurred in student work has a greater chance of being effective because of the source of the instruction.

Since much of how traditional classrooms function is reinforced by the current standards movement, students are indirectly acculturated by the system of education. The result is that those qualities that lead to a child being labeled a *good student* are often characteristics that are least desirable in authentic learning. Scheele (2004) explains that for most students, "We've all been conditioned to wait for things to happen to us instead of making things happen." We don't have to think too deeply to connect Scheele's good-student pattern—"Find out what is expected. Do it. Wait for response"—to how we traditionally and currently teach writing. This purely academic approach to learning is inauthentic and counter to the needs of an individual and the democratic society she is a part of.

Many have known first- or second-hand of entering college and having the type of writing that earned A's in high school severely denounced. While doing research for another book, I came across several news reports to this effect; students who excelled in high school and received top scores on state assessments of writing were being placed in remedial writing courses in college. Some have even left college primarily because of the gap between what they thought were good writing habits and what college writing expects. Original thought and purposeful form are the hallmarks of good writing. The standards movement and high-stakes testing are supporting neither.

When all the outside forces are pushing us to worst practice, we must work doubly hard to avoid that trap—and we must work just as hard not to lay that trap for our students. Now, if we are to teach writing as we know we should, what do we do to implement best practice in writing instruction under the worst possible circumstances? These concerns should guide us.

- We must implement rubrics cautiously, avoiding the worst results of rubric-driven writing assignments and assessments. Popham (2003) offers one of the best and most precise explanations of fashioning rubrics that support authentic writing: essentially, rubrics should avoid two common problems—providing guidelines that are too broad to be of any value or providing guidelines with such detail that the rubric is in essence a template, leading to fill-in-the-blank essays. Effective rubrics are instructionally focused and clear without being prescriptive. For example, a rubric may focus a writing assignment on figurative language; thus, the writing exercise would have as its goal the effective use of figurative language, and the student grade would reflect primarily the use of figurative language.

  Additionally, we might have to include in our instruction the worst kinds of rubrics on occasion in order to prepare our students for standardized test situations that include them. But we must clarify the difference for our students. A type of rubric I have been experimenting with incorporates a series of questions with a scale of scores for each question. The questions can both guide the student during writing and the teacher during assessment, but each question allows great variety and authenticity that identify directly the characteristics needed in a particular piece of writing.

- We must also offer and use sample essays and model passages cautiously. Again, as with rubrics, sample essays and model passages can be highly effective tools, but they can become templates as well. Sample essays and model passages are best used in writing exercises when dealing with focused objectives. Pull a passage from Sandra Cisneros that incorporates vivid verbs to help students focus on their verb choices in their own writing, or pull a paragraph from Joyce Carol Oates and have students mimic her sentence variety in a writing exercise. Sample student essays serve us well also, but we have to state directly and read our student work carefully to avoid students mimicking those samples as if that is the only way to write.

- Since both students and teachers are being held accountable under federal and state mandates that are linked to high-stakes testing, we are obligated to prepare students well even for the worst possible tests! The best way to maintain an authentic and effective writing program under these circumstances is to include in that writing program *test writing* as a separate genre. Just as the Italian sonnet conforms to conventions in a different way than the English sonnet, the prompt-driven test essay is a different animal than the personal essay written by choice in writer's workshop. *Above all else, however, we must never allow preparing our students for standardized assessments of writing to become the entire writing program.*

- We must not allow isolated assessment formats to drive writing instruction. Periodically, the testing machine allows multiple-choice testing of surface features to be called "writing" assessment; we are seeing it again with the revised SAT (2005). *That the assessment format deals with writing elements in isolated and inauthentic ways does not mean that instruction should be isolated and inauthentic.* We must continue to teach grammar, mechanics, and usage in the context of student writing—particularly through targeted writing exercises that offer students well-crafted rubrics. We can deal with those surface features by having students write original pieces that mimic passages in style and technique. At some point close to the actual assessment, we should also expose students to the isolated format of the assessment and directly help students transfer their holistic understandings of the language into isolated situations. But, again, we cannot allow inauthentic tests *to become the instruction*—especially when that format inhibits student understanding and performances.

- We must implement computers cautiously in our writing classes as well. Since computer programs—even basic word processors—are quite able to identify surface feature concerns in student writing, there is a danger that computer-aided writing instruction and assessment could *increase* the disproportionate value placed on surface features at the expense of the writing process and the content of authentic student writing. Further, computer writing programs that assess writing can easily encourage the reduction of all writing to templates to the most inauthentic forms that we are often guilty of emphasizing and to the exclusion of genuine forms when we become too focused on the test instead of the whole writing program.

- We must be aware of who designs the computer writing programs and how those programs are designed, since the programs themselves can ultimately dictate what matters in writing instruction and assessment. We must be certain that the content endorsed by computer writing programs—when they are highly correlated with the standards and high-stakes testing movement—properly reflects authentic writing. Experts in the field of writing must determine what the computer programs say about writing; if that is left to the programmers and the testing experts, writing instruction is doomed.

- We must not allow the ease and speed of computer-aided writing assessment to detract from the quality of writing instruction; without our checking the system, it is entirely possible that high-stakes tests could create highly superficial writing instruction *that conforms well to the assessment process* but actually erodes the quality of writing instruction. In fact, high-stakes tests are already doing so without the impact of computer assessment as shown by Hillocks (2003), Mabry (1999), and Freedman (1991, 1995).

- We must insure that the human element remains the dominant factor in the assessing of student writing. The teachers quoted in Hurwitz's article discussing computer-graded student writing in Indiana clearly raised some key points about the ability of computers to assess. How can a computer determine accuracy, originality, valuable elaboration, empty language, language maturity, and a long list of similar qualities that are central to assessing writing? They can't. We must ultimately and publicly refute the assessing of writing by computers alone.

- We must be very cautious about investing large sums of money into computer hardware and software; the benefits of computers in the writing program and in the entire school program must be weighed and considered carefully. *Though technology can be a wonderful thing, it has never been and will never be a panacea.*

- We should use the benefits of computers and word processors to our advantage. Word processors can be very effective in spelling and surface feature issues if we make the students consider the underlined words or situations in order to make decisions as writers.

- Finally, we must acknowledge that technology can always increase the gaps that exist in our society concerning access to knowledge due to wealth—or the lack of it. If computers and programs are distributed fairly throughout a student population and if we can insure that more affluent students don't receive a technological advantage from their access to technology at home, then the use of computers to aid writing instruction and assessment can serve us well. If, however, the situation further stratifies our students, it must be avoided.

At one point in the not-so-distant past, writing instruction was essentially ignored—especially in high-stakes testing that focused primarily on reading and math. The recent focus on writing that began about twenty years ago is both a curse and a blessing. We are now at least acknowledging the need for and value of writing instruction; however, as writing is co-opted into the standards and high-stakes testing mania, it is being corrupted just as reading and math have been for decades.

Yes, we should work to stop the negative impact that this standards movement is having on writing instruction, but until we can stop the avalanche, we can maintain the integrity of an effective writing program while also preparing our students for the worst of tests.

Reconsidering the Discussion So Far

So: this chapter has, in effect, stated that high-stakes testing and standards don't matter—and that yet they do matter. True.

The most important issue I have addressed here is that the accountability movement has had and will continue to have a profound impact on the content areas that are assessed; writing is quickly being pulled into that category. The research on that dynamic shows primarily negative results on the quality of both writing instruction and writing assessment. The time is now for reassessing the assessments.

The irony here is that writing has finally gained the value it deserves in school, but we must insure that it isn't destroyed in the process. With the help of NWP and NCTE, teachers can become highly effective writing teachers; they can also insure that students perform well on high-stakes assessments of writing even when the tests themselves are flawed.

Glossary

standards—In education, standards refer to the curriculum that has been identified by some agency as the official curriculum of a grade, a course, or a content area. Those standards are often linked to official assessments to identify student achievement in relationship to those standards.

CHAPTER FIVE

Conclusion
The Writer's Life—
Self, Scholar, Writer, Teacher

"If writing is important, adults should be doing it too," Zemelman, Daniels, and Hyde (1998, p. 57) assert in their discussion of best practice in writing instruction. Ultimately, we cannot escape this reality—the best teachers of writing must have some sense of the writer's life themselves. Of course, *becoming* a writer can take distinctly different courses, all of which serve teachers of writing well.

Two decades ago, I fell into a friendship-by-mail with a freelance writer, Peter Nye, who had written a book about the history of American bicycling, another passion of mine. He often wrote to me that writing is something you *have* to do; it is a drive that comes from inside. He reminded me often that *if* I truly am a writer, I will continue to write regardless of the success I encountered in having my work published. What he was referring to is those of us who are born writers, a state that is somewhere between a gift and a curse. I write because I *have* to. With his input, I wrote an entire novel in the 1980s with no real promise of it being published (it never was; all of my book publications have been nonfiction); I wrote it because it demanded to be written.

And yet, I also believe that writers can be made. All of us who teach writing must become writers if we are not already driven to be writers. Everyone who teaches has some background in writing through their academic lives. Many of us never become fully engaged in writing by choice, however, and when we become full-time teachers, we rarely if ever write unless we enroll in graduate courses to renew our teaching certificates. ELA teachers in particular are in the ideal situation to reverse that trend and find opportunities and purposes to become writers themselves—both as an enhancement of their profession and as a valuable part of their lives beyond school.

The thing that we need most to be effective teachers of writing is an intimate experience of the writing life—and we must take that back to our classrooms as well. Those of us who have never lived the writer's life have missed it primarily because we were never properly taught how to write or how to teach others to write. The history of writing instruction has been dominated by worst practice and neglect.

Even for English education majors, the direct and rich teaching of writing has been notably absent. In college-level courses, even English courses, we have been assigned writing often, but we have rarely been given direct and fruitful writing instruction. How many of us have been a part of a writing workshop ourselves such the one I discussed in Chapter Three? Beyond the absence of direct writing instruction for us as students, we have virtually no direct instruction in teaching others to write. Much of learning to write and learning to teach writing has been left to chance.

My own path to the writer's life, however, was punctuated by a high school English teacher who was the first person to assign me real writing; I discovered in his class that I am a lover of books and that I am a writer—because we actually read and we actually wrote. The key was that he had me write, had me compose a variety of works from school essays to poems and fiction. In undergraduate courses, I came across one professor, Dr. Predmore, who challenged every word I wrote—marking my papers in nearly transparent *pencil*—and another professor, Dr. Moore, who praised me as a writer and a poet, encouraging me at every step. Graduate school gave the greatest gift; *every* professor expected me to be both a scholar and a writer. In doing so, they opened my eyes to the broad range of writing that exists at the scholarly level.

Although I believe deeply that my experiences were fortunate ones, what I received as a student amounted more to having rich experiences in being assigned writing or in being expected to be a writer than in having solid instruction on becoming a writer and a teacher of writing. I have spent a great deal of my own life chasing down how to be a better writer and a better teacher of writing. One touchstone throughout that journey has been the Spartanburg Writing Project (SWP); as an affiliate of the NWP, the SWP gave me both the instruction and experiences I needed as a writer and a teacher of writers through workshop experiences where I practiced being a writer and a teacher of writing among experts in the field as well as my peers.

I tell this story of my journey because my experience is relatively unusual. For some inexplicable reason, I am called to be a writer, *and* I happened upon a series of wonderful teachers who both taught me well, though often indirectly, to be a writer and to teach others to write. *But most ELA teachers have had neither experience; they do not feel called to write and their preparation as writers and teachers of writers are notably lacking.* I make this claim simply to say that all of us should and can enter the writing life. This chapter will discuss how to find the writing life, both as rewarding personal and professional experiences.

The Writer's Life

Tim O'Brien (1999) explains that he has a daily writing schedule that is very much a self-imposed, all-day routine that rivals traditional nine-to-five work schedules; he admits that "even when I'm . . . [lifting weights], I'm still writing in my head." I write nearly every day of the workweek and occasionally on weekends; my schedule is much less structured than O'Brien's, but I share one facet with him—I am *always* writing in my head. I drafted the beginning to this chapter in the shower on the morning that I first typed these words into my word processor. From writers whose primary profession is writing, to people such as I who write within a broader profession, the experience that I am describing is the writing life.

The writing life can take many forms and many purposes, which I will discuss here, but the qualities that most distinguish the writing life are *routine* and *purpose*. As you begin exploring or building *your* writing life, you will discover these for yourself. To facilitate this discussion, I have divided the writing life into four categories—writing for self, writing to speak to the broader community, writing to express, and writing to publish.

One avenue to the writing life is writing for your "Self"— often in the form of keeping a journal or diary. Franz Kafka wrote voluminous journal entries throughout his life; he is a perfect example of those people driven to write. In fact, Kafka seems to have cared little for having an audience, even requesting that his unpublished works be destroyed when he died. For many of us who teach, the writing life will take the form of daily— or near daily—journaling or writing of diary entries. This is a kind of putting our lives on paper. Many people find it highly rewarding to buy a journal and begin writing—with the act of selecting and buying a journal adding to the experience.

Keeping a journal or diary may be either the whole of your writing life or part of a larger writing life; either form is an excellent source of improving your role as a writing teacher. Especially if keeping a journal or diary is the whole of your writing life, I suggest that you establish a schedule that you keep with a high degree of dedication. A daily schedule would be best, but any regular schedule will make both the writing experience and the value that experience contributes to you as a teacher deeper and more effective. A journal (a special place to write *in*), a schedule, and a designated *place* to write will help make your writing life something that is meaningful to you as a person, a writer, and a teacher.

The act of writing is an act of reflection and an act of discovery—as others have noted in previous chapters. Once you as a teacher have experienced the value in keeping a journal, you have a source for sharing with students. That sharing can take the form of reading from your journal, talking about a journal entry, or discussing with students the results of keeping a journal. Using the journal for *you* is a first step; next, this form of the writing life needs to become a part of you as teacher, so that your students see you as both a teacher and as a writer.

Another type of the writing life is writing that speaks to the broader community through writing letters to the editor of local papers or magazines and journals, writing guest Op-Ed pieces for local newspapers, and writing letters to those in power—from politicians to pundits. Writing with purpose, we have found through research, is one of the most significant aspects of the writing life; as well, most educational thinkers believe that education is a central part of the democratic process, which requires dialogue among those within that democracy. As an example of living the writing life, writing with purpose, and contributing to the democratic discourse, writing teachers can make a profound impact by raising their voices as writers who are also professional educators. A well-constructed letter to the editor or guest Op-Ed article can go a long way towards raising the level of a teacher's professionalism, her credibility as a writer and thinker, and her significant role in the democratic process. Letters to journals and magazines can serve the same purpose. Further, well-crafted letters to people in power can speak volumes.

As a teacher and as a teacher who writes, you should begin to seek avenues for sharing your voice through writing. Part of the writing life often involves seeking proper audiences; for students, seeing the interplay between purpose, audience, and writer in the form of the teacher gives your lessons on writing a weight and reality that few other situations can.

Again, as a citizen and as an educator, each teacher should contribute her voice to our leaders, especially our political leaders, through putting words to paper. While journaling is a personal journey through words, sharing one's self publicly through words is one of the most powerful forms of participating in the greater society—especially our society, a democracy that depends on dialogue and the sharing of ideas through words. During my years as a public school teacher, I was consistently impressed with how my students and their parents responded to my simply having a letter to the editor in the local paper. That act of public expression should never be underestimated as a model for our students of both the power of language and our participation in a democratic society.

A third aspect of the writer's life involves what most people call creative writing—poetry, fiction, memoirs and autobiography, and creative nonfiction. I recently taught a course for middle school ELA teachers, a course that offered what was for most of them the first opportunity to live the writer's life. We began each day with a morning reading and at least an hour of writing time where those teachers wrote by choice and with purpose. One teacher expressed her concern for losing that hour of writing time when the course ended. When I suggested that she might begin keeping a diary or journal, she explained that journaling had never appealed to her; she feared losing the time to write creatively.

Like her, I have never been able to keep a writer's journal—though I consider myself a writer and write virtually every day. Many of us feel a need to be creative, and creative writing is a perfect outlet for that drive. The writing of work that we call "creative"—a term redefined by LaBrant (1936) to mean writing that is characterized by the writer having choice in the topic, form, and length of any piece—fulfills our need for autonomy, but I would add to LaBrant's parameters that creative writing offers one quality beyond journaling that is directly related to our roles as writers *and* teachers—craft.

When we keep a diary or a journal, we often write to learn, to come to terms with our lives and our selves. We are the audience, and the simple drafting often fulfills our needs during the journaling. When we move that writing from journaling to creative writing, two significant changes occur; we become concerned with an *audience* and with the actual craft of the sentences—from word choice to syntax to figurative language. The diary or journal is notable for the spontaneity of the writing, the immediacy of a single draft. But creative writing moves beyond simple expression to the craft of expressing. We look closely at the *what* in our writing and the *how* of our writing—writing a single piece over a number of drafts.

For a teacher of writing, having regular experiences with the craft of writing is crucial. The craft of writing forces a writer to consider carefully and *holistically* (not just what each element is and does, but how the elements all impact each other and the message of the writing) all the aspects of writing that we have to address as teachers—surface features, literary elements, audience, form, syntax, diction, etc. Yes, as experienced readers of highly sophisticated literature, we can teach writing by transferring our knowledge of other writers to student work, but when we have lived this process ourselves, our effectiveness is greatly enhanced.

Just as keeping a journal and writing to the broader public offer excellent opportunities to bring those experiences into the classroom to support instruction, creative writing by a teacher provides many opportunities for the classroom. In the summer course I mentioned above, the ELA teachers found that through their writing, they had final drafts of pieces to share with their students (ones that allowed them to discuss purpose, craft, and process authentically); they had multiple drafts of pieces to bring the writing process to life, and they had the ability to discuss with their students the elements of their own writing process—one discovered during the summer workshop. These teachers left that class excited about having had real experiences with drafting and crafting—for many a first-time experience.

The final aspect of a writer's life is writing to publish— sometimes as an outlet for scholarship and sometimes as a part of the process of writing. The authentic writing process—one that is unique to each writer, one that each writer has to discover and refine herself— leads to publishing or at least a draft that is submitted for publishing. Just as moving from journaling to creative writing brings in a concern for audience and craft, the added element of publishing changes the work of the writer. On a smaller scale, our earlier discussion about submitting letters to the editor or guest Op-Ed pieces provides writers with the most accessible avenues to being a published writer. Once a writer enters the world of submitting writing for publication, yet another aspect of living the writer's life is added.

Submitting work to journals, magazines, and book publishers is nearly an art in itself. Both teachers and students can benefit greatly from adding the submission process to the writing process. For a teacher, deciding to submit work for publication is also a key step in raising the level of scholarship in the field. While becoming a published poet, novelist, or writer of short fiction can be nearly impossible, seeing professional pieces or nonfiction articles in print is very much achievable for those of us who commit ourselves to being published. To begin submitting work for publication, a writer must consider these concerns.

- Submitting work for publication creates a unique concern for the final formatting of a piece of writing. Those formatting concerns become dictated by the guidelines of the journal, magazine, or publisher where the piece will be submitted. In most classrooms, the submission process is inauthentic; simply turning in an essay and fulfilling the requirements of a teacher often feels hollow to all of us who have sat in classrooms as students. For a teacher *and* a student, having a real purpose for formatting concerns brings urgency to setting margins, determining fonts and font sizes, selecting paper stock, and fulfilling the requirements of the documentation format required by the editors. Nothing helps a writer gain an appreciation for and understanding of documentation style sheets better than submitting work for publication. Moreover, few things are as humbling as having to submit a work for publication in a format that you, as a teacher, have never used before; this process has been eye-opening for me as my English training involved Modern Language Association (MLA) style sheets, but my field of education prefers American Psychological Association (APA) style sheets.

- The greatest impact submitting work has on the act of composing is that when we decide to submit work for publication we have to be familiar with the needs and wants of the place of publication. This is a unique situation for reading like a writer, a writer who hopes to be published. Before anyone submits a work for publication, she should read and study the publication beforehand if at all possible, if it is a journal or magazine. If a writer is submitting work based on a call for papers for a new book or publication or submitting a book-length manuscript to a publisher, he should do as much research as possible, including contacting the editors for clarifications and submitting detailed proposals or initial letters explaining what the writer believes is appropriate for the call.

- Once a writer commits to submitting work for publication, she needs to begin working with others to craft her manuscript. A friendly but sharp manuscript reader or two is invaluable, but when a writer submits work, she often gains a wonderful experience—working with editors. I have gained so much from editors that I could not name all of the lessons here. Most editors are incredibly supportive and master writers themselves. When a writer submits work for publication, she is becoming part of a larger writing purpose—that purposefulness among several writers and editors being the most authentic experience a writer can discover.

- It is worth elaborating upon the importance of documentation formats and style sheets when submitting work for publication as mentioned above. Too many of us during our teaching career have known documentation only as a requirement of research papers—or for many of us, "term" papers—that is, only as a part of an academic assignment. For those of us in the field of ELA, we have been working with the guidelines of the MLA, but we may have little experience with the other formats that many fields and publications require—notably from the APA or the *Chicago Manual of Style*. When a writer begins submitting work, however, he soon learns than no matter what format a journal or editor requires, some unique requirements may also exist; for many years, guidelines for the *English Journal* called for a modified MLA format. What submitting a work teaches a writer is the ability to conform to the requirements, regardless of what those requirements are.

Ultimately, the writing teacher must adopt some form of the writing life to be an effective writing teacher. Over the course of a life, many of us may move among the lives I have discussed above as our careers and needs shift. Nothing has enhanced my life as a person and as a teacher more than my journey as a writer, and that guides my call for all writing teachers to be writers. To echo the sentiment that begins this chapter, the best way to show our students that the lessons of our courses matter is that we live the life we teach.

A Community of Writers

The writing life inevitably leads to becoming a part of a community of writers—paralleling the community that is at the center of workshop approaches to instruction. The NWP is probably the single most successful source of creating communities of writers and promoting teacher scholarship through writing. For a writing teacher who decides to adopt the writing life, it is an added call to either create or join a community of writers.

Beyond simply beginning to submit work for publication, teachers looking for a community of writers should seek out a local affiliate of the NWP—easily found on the NWP web site—usually working with a local college or university. Summer institutes, leadership teams, and a wide array of other programs grow out of NWP affiliates and offer teachers an ideal setting for professional and personal growth. The greatest value to NWP affiliates is that their philosophy embraces the growth of teachers as both writers and teachers of emphasizing that the two are inseparable.

Other avenues to communities of writers exist as well. Writing clubs affiliated with local colleges or universities and local bookstores are usually open to new members. A teacher's own classroom or ELA department offers an excellent opportunity to form a writing community with nearly daily access. In our electronic age, the Internet also provides a source of community for writers, both for joining a community or forming one.

Reconsidering the Discussion So Far

While I firmly believe the primary argument of this chapter, many will argue that writing teachers don't have to be writers. I concede that possibility. But I have too much evidence supporting my position to give in. At the very least, we should be writing with our students in our classes.

What does it mean that writing teachers should be writers? I believe we must encourage each other to begin demanding opportunities to grow as writers and teachers of writing through the coursework we take in graduate classes and through the broader school communities within which we teach. At the college level, professors are expected to be scholars and writers; this tradition encourages some wonderful qualities for professors. At the public school level, I believe we can begin that same tradition. Both students and teachers will benefit from it.

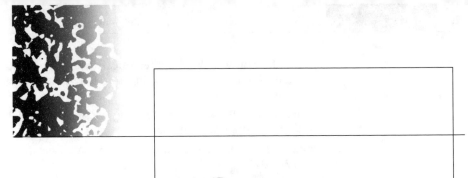

References
and Resources

Adler, K. (2004, April 25). Professor's tips on writing right. *San Antonio Express-News*.

Allington, R. L. (2004). Setting the record straight. *Educational Leadership, 61* (6), 22–25.

Armstrong, T. (2003). *The multiple intelligences of reading and writing: Making the words come alive*. Alexandria, VA: Association for Supervision and Curriculum Development.

Atwell, N. (1998). *In the Middle: New understanding about writing, reading, and learning* (2nd ed.). Portsmouth, NH: Boynton/Cook.

Barzun, J. (1991). *Begin here: The forgotten conditions of teaching and learning*. Chicago: The University of Chicago Press.

Brooks, J. G., & Brooks, M. G. (1999). *In search of understanding: The case for constructivist classrooms*. Alexandria, VA: Association for Supervision and Curriculum Development.

Calfee, R. (1994a). Ahead to the past: Assessing student achievement in writing. National Center for the Study of Writing Occasional Paper No. 39. Available on-line at www.writingproject.org/Resources/techreports.html

————. (1994b). Implications of cognitive psychology for authentic assessment and instruction. National Center for the Study of Writing Technical Report No. 69. Available on-line at www.writingproject.org/Resources/techreports.html

Calkins, L. M. (1994). *The art of teaching writing* (2nd ed.). Portsmouth, NH: Heinemann.

Cloud, J. (2003, October 27). Inside the new SAT. *Time, 162* (17), 48–56.

Dell'Angela, T. (2004, June 15). State has a strange way with words. *Chicago Tribune*. Retrieved June 16, 2004, from: www.chicagotribune.com.

Fletcher, R. (1993). *What a writer needs*. Portsmouth, NH: Heinemann.

Flippo, R. F. (2003). *Assessing readers: Qualitative diagnosis and instruction*. Portsmouth, NH: Heinemann.

Freedman, S. W. (1991). Evaluating writing: Linking large-scale testing and classroom assessment. National Center for the Study of Writing Occasional Paper No. 27. Available on-line at www.writingproject.org/Resources/techreports.html

———. (1995). Exam-based reform stifles student writing in the U.K. *Educational Leadership, 52* (6), 26–29.

Freedman, S. W., Dyson, A. H., Flower, L., & Chafe, W. (1987). Research in writing: Past, present, and future. National Center for the Study of Writing Technical Report No. 1. Available on-line at www.writingproject.org/Resources/techreports.html

Freedman, S. W., Flower, L., Hull, G., & Hayes, J. R. (1995). Ten years of research: Achievements of the National Center for the Study of Writing. National Center for the Study of Writing Technical Report No. 1-C. Available on-line at www.writingproject.org/Resources/techreports.html

Freedman, S. W., & Hechinger, F. (1992). Writing matters. National Center for the Study of Writing Occasional Paper No. 31. Available on-line at www.writingproject.org/Resources/techreports.html

Freire, P. (1993). Pedagogy of the oppressed. New York: Continuum.

Gardner, J. (1991). *The art of fiction: Notes on craft for young writers*. New York: Vintage Books.

———. (1999). *On becoming a novelist*. New York: W. W. Norton and Co.

Garner, D. (2004, May 28). The bottomline on the spring TAKS scores. *EducationNews.org*. Retrieved June 2, 2004, from: www.educationnews.org/bottomline-on-the-spring-taks.htm

Greene, M. (1995). *Releasing the imagination: Essays on education, the arts, and social change.* San Francisco: Jossey-Bass.

Hillocks, G., Jr. (2003). Fighting back: Assessing the assessments. *English Journal, 2* (4), 63–70.

———. (1995). *Teaching writing as reflective practice.* New York: Teachers College Press.

hooks, b. (1999). *remembered rapture: the writer at work.* New York: Henry Holt and Company.

———. (1994). Teaching to transgress: Education as the practice of freedom. New York: Routledge.

Hurwitz, S. (2004, May 19). Indiana essays being graded by computers. New York Times. Retrieved May 19, 2004, from: www.nytimes.com.

Hurwitz, N., & Hurwitz, S. (2004). Words on paper. American School Board Journal, 191 (3). Retrieved March 8, 2004, from: www.asbj.com.

Jago, C. (2001). *Beyond standards: Excellence in the high school classroom.* Portsmouth, NH: Heinemann.

———. (2002). *Cohesive writing: Why concept is not enough.* Portsmouth, NH: Heinemann.

Kohn, A. (1996). *Beyond discipline: From compliance to community.* Alexandria, VA: Association for Supervision and Curriculum Development.

Krashen, S. (2004). False claims about literacy development. *Educational Leadership, 61* (6), 18–21.

LaBrant, L. (1949). Analysis of clichés and abstractions. *English Journal, 38* (5), 275–278.

———. . (1959). As of now. *English Journal, 48* (6), 295–303.

———. (1934). The changing sentence structure of children. *The Elementary English Review, 11* (3), 59–65, 86.

———. (1950). The individual and his writing. *English Journal, 39* (4), 185–189.

———. (1955). Inducing students to write. *English Journal, 44* (2), 70–74, 116.

———. (1943). Language teaching in a changing world. *The Elementary English Review, 20* (3), 93–97.

———. (1964). Teaching English: A choice. *Louisiana English Journal, 5* (1), 34–37.

———. (1952a). New bottles for new wine. *English Journal, 41* (7), 341–347.

———. (1936). The psychological basis for creative writing. *English Journal, 25* (4), 292–301.

———. (1947). Research in language. *Elementary English, 24* (2), 86–94.

———. (1952b). Some implications of research for the teaching of oral and written composition. In A. E. Traxler (Ed.), *Education in a period of national preparedness* (pp. 123–131). Washington, DC: American Council on Education.

———. (1946). Teaching high-school students to write. *English Journal, 35* (3), 123–128.

———. (1953). Writing is learned by writing. *Elementary English, 30* (7), 417–420.

———. (1957). Writing is more than structure. *English Journal, 46* (5), 252–256, 293.

Langer, J. A. (2002). *Effective literacy instruction: Building successful reading and writing programs.* Urbana, IL: National Council of Teachers of English.

Mabry, L. (1999, May). Writing to the rubric: Lingering effects of traditional standardized testing on direct writing assessment. *Phi Delta Kappan, 80* (9), 673–679.

Markley, M. (2004, June 6). TAAS scores rose as SATs fell. *Houston Chronicle.* Retrieved June 15, 2004, from: www.chron.com.

National Center for Educational Statistics. (2002). Writing 2002 major results. Retrieved July 10, 2003, from: nces.ed.gov/nationsreportcard/writing/results2002/.

National Commission on Writing in America's Schools and Colleges (2003, April). The neglected "R": The need for a writing revolution. New York: The College Board. Available on-line at www.writingcommission.org/.

Noskin, D. P. (2000). Teaching writing in the high school: Fifteen years in the making. English Journal, 90 (1), 34–38.

O'Brien, T. (1999, April 21). Writing Vietnam. President's Lecture. Retrieved April 23, 2004, from: www.stg.brown.edu/projects/WritingVietnam/obrien.html

Pinker, S. (1994). *The language instinct.* New York: Harper Perennial.

———. (1999). *Words and rules: The ingredients of language.* New York: Basic Books.

Popham, W. J. (2003). *Test better, teach better: The instructional role of assessment.* Alexandria, VA: Association for Supervision and Curriculum Development.

Ray, K. W., & Laminack, L. L. (2001). *The writing workshop: Working through the hard parts (and they're all hard parts).* Urbana, IL: National Council of Teachers of English.

Reeves, D. B. (2004). *Accountability for learning: How teachers and school leaders can take charge.* Alexandria, VA: Association for Supervision and Curriculum Development.

Riley, C. (2004, June 15). State may issue tests on school computers. *Tennessean.* Retrieved June 16, 2004, from: cgi.tennessean.com.

Rosenblatt, L. M. (1988). Writing and reading: The transactional theory. National Center for the Study of Writing Technical Report No. 13. Available on-line at www.writingproject.org/Resources/techreports.html

Routman, R. (1996). *Literacy at the crossroads: Crucial talk about reading, writing, and other teaching dilemmas.* Portsmouth, NH: Heinemann.

———. (2004). *Writing essentials: Raising expectations and results while simplifying teaching.* Portsmouth, NH: Heinemann.

Sartwell, C. (2004, May 20). The lobotomized weasel school of writing. *Los Angeles Times.* Retrieved May 24, 2004, from: www.latimes.com

Scheele, A. (2004, May 6). The good student trap. *Washington Post.* Retrieved May 10, 2004, from: www.washingtonpost.com

Thomas, P. (2001a). *Lou LaBrant—A woman's life, a teacher's life.* Huntington, NY: Nova Science Publishers, Inc.

Thomas, P. L. (2000a). Blueprints or houses? Lou LaBrant and the writing debate. *English Journal, 89* (3), 85–89.

———. (2000b). The struggle itself: Teaching writing as we know we should. *English Journal, 90* (1), 39–45.

———. (2001b). *Vivid language: Writer as reader, reader as writer.* Lanham, MD: University Press of America.

Vonnegut, K. (1974). Teaching the unteachable. *Wampeters, foam, and granfalloons.* New York: Delta.

Walzer, P. (2004, June 9). Maury style lasts, write or wrong. *The Virginian-Pilot.* Retrieved June 16, 2004, from: home.hamptonroads.com.

Weaver, C., ed. (1998). *Lessons to share on teaching grammar in context.* Portsmouth, NH: Heinemann.

———. (1996). *Teaching grammar in context.* Portsmouth, NH: Heinemann.

Weiss, I. R., & Pasley, J. D. (2004). What is high-quality instruction? *Educational Leadership, 61* (5), 24–28.

Williams, J. M. (1997). *Style: Ten lessons in clarity and grace* (5th ed.). New York: Longman.

———. (1990). *Style: Toward clarity and grace.* Chicago: The University of Chicago Press.

Zemelman, S., Daniels, H., & Hyde, A. (1998). *Best Practice: New standards for teaching and learning in America's schools* (2nd ed.). Portsmouth, NH: Heinemann.

Zinsser, W. (2001). *On writing well: The classic guide to writing nonfiction* (25th Anniversary Edition). New York: Quill.

Teachers and Writers—Those to Consider

Atwell, Nancie

Calkins, Lucy

Fletcher, Ralph

Fox, Mem

Gardner, John

Graves, Donald

Hillocks, Jr., George

Jago, Carol

Laminack, Lester

Murray, Donald

Ray, Katie Wood

Routman, Regie

Strunk, Jr, William

Weaver, Constance

White, E. B.

Williams, Joseph

Zinsser, William

Organizations

National Center for the Study of Writing (see NWP web page www.writingproject.org)

National Commission on Writing in America's Schools and Colleges (www.collegeboard.com)

National Council of Teachers of English (NCTE) (www.ncte.org)

National Writing Project (NWP) (www.writingproject.org)

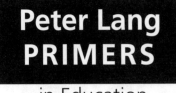

in Education

Peter Lang Primers are designed to provide a brief and concise introduction or supplement to specific topics in education. Although sophisticated in content, these primers are written in an accessible style, making them perfect for undergraduate and graduate classroom use. Each volume includes a glossary of key terms and a References and Resources section.

Other published and forthcoming volumes cover such topics as:
- Standards
- Popular Culture
- Critical Pedagogy
- Literacy
- Higher Education
- John Dewey
- Feminist Theory and Education
- Studying Urban Youth Culture
- Multiculturalism through Postformalism
- Creative Problem Solving
- Teaching the Holocaust
- Piaget and Education
- Deleuze and Education
- Foucault and Education

Look for more Peter Lang Primers to be published soon. To order other volumes, please contact our Customer Service Department:

      800-770-LANG (within the US)
      212-647-7706 (outside the US)
      212-647-7707 (fax)

To find out more about this and other Peter Lang book series, or to browse a full list of education titles, please visit our website:

      www.peterlangusa.com